THE
LITTLE
BOOK
OF
THREADS

Sayre Van Young & Marin Van Young

THE
LITTLE
BOOK
OF
THREADS

1,400 OF THE MOST
POSTABLE QUOTES
OF ALL TIME

Previously published as *Tweet This Book*

Published by:
Ulysses Press
PO Box 3440
Berkeley, CA 94703
www.ulyssespress.com

ISBN: 978-1-64604-663-8
Library of Congress Control Number: 2023943686

Printed in the United States
10 9 8 7 6 5 4 3 2 1

Acquisitions editor: Kelly Reed
Managing editor: Claire Chun
Editors: Lauren Harrison, Renee Rutledge
Cover design: Keith Riegert
Cover illustration: © Tally18/shutterstock; Oscar Wilde
    © Natata/shutterstock
Production: Yesenia Garcia-Lopez

Dedication:
Thank you...you know who you are.
—*Anonymous*

Contents

Acknowledgments

...for which I pay 'em a thousand thanks...

William Shakespeare

Our thanks to Will Marston and Susan Huish, for suggesting some great Dumb...Dumber...Dumbest lines; to Andrea Mullarky and Carole Leita for offering some Words to Live By; to Ethel Manheimer and Sunny Adler for providing several of their (and our) favorite quotes; to Wendie Vermillion for a quote that kept us going; to Cathy McAuliffe and Anita Schriver, for support and encouragement... and some great meals together. The Ulysses folks were and are wonderful to work with—especially Kelly Reed (who got us into this), Lauren Harrison (who kept us from embarrassing ourselves), Judith Metzener (who made it all read well), and Claire Chun (who, as usual, held everything together).

And as always, our grateful thanks to Diane Davenport. Words fail us.

Introduction

> A proper collection of quotations is the whole world digested.
> *Terri Guillemets*

In writing this book, we figured a "greatest" quote is something like "Fourscore and seven years ago." But it turns out that a lot of great quotes just aren't very tweetable. Either they're too long-windedly noble ("We hold these truths to be self-evident") or they lose their nobility by shortening ("2 B or not 2 B"). So we broadened our definition.

We thought of those moments when the perfect quote would come in handy, something to describe what we're thinking, wishing, needing, avoiding, forgetting, or seeing. And then we went out and collected the pithy wisdom of everyone from Plato to Monty Python.

In these pages, yu'll find plenty of grand social topics like Art, Consistency, Loneliness, Marriage, and Simplicity. But you'll also find comments about daily life: bitching and moaning, cell phones, clutter, dieting, naps, traffic, finding a bathroom—and dozens of other subjects.

As to the arrangement of all these wise nuggets—really, where would you put a quote like "After all, computers crash, people die, relationships fall apart. The best we can do is breathe and reboot." Technology? Death? Relationships? Persistence? We used our best judgment and counted on your willingness to wander.

Incidentally, there are a bazillion quote books out there. The print ones we depended on are in the Bibliography (as are some great websites). And if 1,400 quotes aren't enough and you head to the books, be forewarned: They're arranged by exciting topics like Agriculture or Founding Fathers or Urban Affairs, which are great for term papers, but not so great for life—or social media.

Every quote here is perfectly succinct for the most effective social media posts. And some text and names have been shortened to make them a bit more to the point. After all, do you really need to know that Goethe's full name is Johann Wolfgang von Goethe? We thought not.

Speaking of giving credit—many people have said many of the same great things, sometimes so many that the only possible way to credit the quote is "Anonymous." For movies and TV shows, we've credited the speaker, not the screenwriter; for plays and books, we've credited the author.

Now we've come to the end of our lengthy ramble. Don't worry, the information in the rest of the book is much more concise. And while these "greatest" quotes may not all be studied in school or spouted in speeches, we hope you'll find some that perfectly express your feelings. After all, when that happens, isn't it the greatest?

—Sayre Van Young and Marin Van Young

***

Acceptance

The concept of "acceptance" is closely related to saying "Whatever," but some of these quotes will bring a little more panache to your posts.

It is what it is.
Anonymous

It'll be what it'll be.
Anonymous

Everyone must row with the oars he has.
English proverb

The sun will set without your help.
Anonymous

To everything there is a season, and a time to every purpose under heaven.
Bible [modified a bit by Pete Seeger]

One cannot collect all the beautiful shells on the beach.
Anne Morrow Lindbergh

Everyone is in the best seat.
John Cage

You're going to have more rejection than acceptance.
Barry Mann

Ya gotta do what ya gotta do.
Sylvester Stallone [in the movie Rocky]

Sometimes a cigar is just a cigar.
Sigmund Freud

Everybody is all right, really.
Winnie the Pooh [A. A. Milne]

Happiness can exist only in acceptance.
George Orwell

Sometimes you just gotta say "what the fuck."
Tom Cruise [in the movie Risky Business]

And that's the way it is.
Walter Cronkite

Adventure See Travel & Adventure

Advice

Advice in General

I always pass on good advice. It is the only thing to do with it. It is never of any use to oneself.

Oscar Wilde

Advice is what we ask for when we already know the answer but wish we didn't.

Erica Jong

The best way to give advice to your children is to find out what they want, and then advise them to do it.

Harry S Truman

Never advise anyone to go to war or to marry.

Spanish proverb

Accept good advice gracefully—as long as it doesn't interfere with what you intended to do in the first place.

Gene Brown

Good advice is often annoying. Bad advice never is.

French proverb

Bad Advice

Do as we say and not as we do.

Giovanni Boccaccio [Use the original Italian for that special touch: Fate quello che noi diciamo e non quello che noi facciamo.]

Damned Good Advice See also Words to Live By

Keep breathing.

Sophie Tucker

Whether you believe you can do a thing or not, you are right.

Henry Ford

Say little and do much.

Talmud

Don't compromise yourself. You are all you've got.

Janis Joplin

Trust in Allah, but tie up your camel.

Arabian proverb

Love your neighbor, but don't pull down the fence.
Swiss/German proverb

Never under any circumstances take a sleeping pill and a laxative on the same night.
Dave Berry

Remember that a kick in the ass is a step forward.
Anonymous

No matter who you are or what you plan to do, learn to type!
Liz Smith

You were born an original. Don't die a copy.
John Mason

Whatever you are, be a good one.
Abraham Lincoln

Never mistake motion for action.
Ernest Hemingway

More hustle, less bustle.
Anonymous

Trust everybody, but cut the cards.
Finley Peter Dunne

When you reach the top, keep climbing.
Zen saying

I always skate to where the puck is going, not where it's been.
Wayne Gretsky

Be yourself. Everyone else is already taken.
Oscar Wilde

Do what you can, with what you have, where you are.
Theodore Roosevelt

Freedom lies in being bold.
Robert Frost

Follow your bliss.
Joseph Campbell

Only dead fish swim with the stream.
Anonymous

Sometimes you have to be a bitch to get things done.
Madonna

Nothing can bring you peace but yourself.
Ralph Waldo Emerson

We make a living by what we get, we make
a life by what we give.
Winston Churchill

If it ain't broke, don't fix it.
Anonymous

Details are always vulgar.
Oscar Wilde

Out of sight, out of mind.
Old English saying

Oh, grow up!
Joan Rivers

Remember—wherever you go, there
you are.
*Anonymous [i.e., said in some form by many,
from Confucius to Buckaroo Banzai]*

Age & Aging

Being Younger

You are only young once, and that excuse won't last forever.

Anonymous

It is better to waste one's youth than to do nothing with it at all.

Georges Courteline

It takes courage to grow up and turn out to be who you really are.

e. e. cummings

The only way to stay young is to avoid older people.

James D. Watson

All would live long, but none would be old.

Benjamin Franklin

Being Older

When I was young I loved truth, justice, and liberty, and now that I'm older I love truth, justice, liberty, and crabmeat.

Anonymous

I recently turned 60. Practically a third of my life is over.

Woody Allen

I have more prescriptions than subscriptions.

Anonymous

Old age is no place for sissies.

Bette Davis [among many others, including Henry Louis Mencken and Art Linkletter]

Middle age is the time when a man is always thinking that in a week or two he will feel as good as ever.

Don Marquis

Old age is always 15 years older than I am.

Bernard Baruch

I've aged…. I'm getting lines in my face. I look like a brand-new, steel-belted radial tire.

Maggie Smith [in the movie California Suite*]*

When you win, you're an old pro. When you lose, you're an old man.

Charlie Conerly

I'm at an age when my back goes out more than I do.

Phyllis Diller

Inside every older person is a younger person wondering what the fuck happened.

Anonymous

One of the delights known to age, and beyond the grasp of youth, is that of Not Going.

J. B. Priestley

Like a fine wine, I'm not getting older, I'm becoming more complex.

Anonymous

Youth vs. Age

Old and young, we are all on our last cruise.

Robert Louis Stevenson

The young sow wild oats, the old grow sage.

Winston Churchill

The old believe everything; the middle-aged suspect everything; the young know everything.
Oscar Wilde

The young man knows the rules, but the old man knows the exceptions.
Oliver Wendell Holmes

Air Travel See Bummer—Flying

Alcohol See Drinks & Drinking

Anger See also Arguments & Fighting

We boil at different degrees.
Ralph Waldo Emerson

Don't get your knickers in a knot. Nothing is solved and it just makes you walk funny.
Kathryn Carpenter

When a man angers you, he conquers you.
Toni Morrison

Please be patient. At the moment I'm too angry to tell you how angry I am.
Ashleigh Brilliant

Anger is only one letter short of danger.
Anonymous

I'm as mad as hell, and I'm not going to take this anymore!
Peter Finch [in the movie Network*]*

The best answer to anger is silence.
Anonymous

No man can think clearly when his fists are clenched.
George Jean Nathan

Anger is a sign that something needs to change.
Mark Epstein

Get mad, then get over it.
Colin Powell

Animals

Cats

There are no ordinary cats.
Colette

Cats invented self-esteem.
Erma Bombeck

Cats don't adopt people. They adopt refrigerators.
Solomon Short

If a cat spoke, it would say things like, "Hey I don't see the *problem* here."
Roy Blount, Jr.

The problem with cats is that they get the exact same look whether they see a moth or an ax murderer.
Paula Poundstone

There is, incidentally, no way of talking about cats that enables one to come off as a sane person.
Dan Greenburg

Dogs

The average dog is a nicer person than the average person.

Andy Rooney

Dogs aren't particularly interested in sticks; what they are interested in is crotches.

Jenny Éclair

Man is a dog's ideal of what God should be.

Holbrook Jackson

A dog's idea of personal grooming is to roll on a dead fish.

James Gorman

No one appreciates the very special genius of your conversation as a dog does.

Christopher Morley

Dogs never lie about love.

Mike Del Ross

Love me, love my dog.

Anonymous

Dogs & Cats

Dogs come when they're called; cats take a message and get back to you later.

Mary Bly

A dog is prose; a cat is a poem.

Jean Burden

Other Animals

The best thing about animals is that they don't talk much.

Thornton Wilder

Did you know a dolphin is just a gay shark?

[from the TV program Glee]

The caterpillar does all the work, but the butterfly gets all the publicity.

George Carlin

Did you know that squirrels are the devil's oven mitts?

Miss Piggy

I like pigs. Dogs look up to us. Cats look down on us. Pigs treat us as equals.

Winston Churchill

Appearance, Personal *See also* Clothes & Fashion

Is that a beard, or are you eating a muskrat?

Dr. Gonzo

Beauty, to me, is about being comfortable in your own skin. That, or a kick-ass red lipstick.

Gwyneth Paltrow

I'm tired of all this nonsense about beauty being only skin-deep. What do you want—an adorable pancreas?

Jean Kerr

If truth is beauty, how come no one has their hair done in the library?

Lily Tomlin

His hair is getting thin—still, who wants fat hair?

Milton Berle

Some of the worst mistakes of my life have been haircuts.

Jim Morrison

Why don't you get a haircut? You look like
a chrysanthemum.
P. G. Wodehouse

Her hair has more body than I do.
Anonymous

Gorgeous hair is the best revenge.
Ivana Trump

If people turn to look at you on the street,
you are not well dressed.
Beau Brummel

It's okay to be fat. So you're fat. Just be fat
and shut up about it.
Roseanne Barr

Let us be grateful to the mirror for
revealing to us our appearance only.
Samuel Butler

Any time I can look a little taller...I'm
happy.
Jennifer Aniston

It's hard to be naked and not to be
upstaged by your nipples.
Susan Sarandon

Never trust a man with short legs. Brains too near their bottoms.
Noël Coward

Beauty comes in all sizes, not just size 5.
Roseanne Barr

It is only shallow people who do not judge by appearances.
Oscar Wilde

Business clothes are naturally attracted to staining liquids. This attraction is strongest just before an important meeting.
Scott Adams

Arguments & Fighting *See also* Anger

Fasten your seat belts. It's going to be a bumpy night.
Bette Davis [in the movie All About Eve*]*

He who slings mud generally loses ground.
Adlai Stevenson

People who fight fire with fire usually end up with ashes.
Abigail Van Buren [aka Dear Abby]

When someone says they don't mind,
they mind.
African-American proverb

Argument is the worst sort of conversation.
Jonathan Swift

Several excuses are always less convincing
than one.
Aldous Huxley

Behind every argument is someone's
ignorance.
Louis Brandeis

I'm not arguing with you—I am telling you.
James McNeill Whistler

Art & Artists

If that's art, I'm a Hottentot.
Harry S. Truman

I work in whatever medium likes me at the
moment.
Marc Chagall

Painting is just another way of keeping a diary.
Pablo Picasso

Great art picks up where nature left off.
Marc Chagall

Creativity is allowing yourself to make mistakes. Art is knowing which ones to keep.
Scott Adams

All children are artists. The problem is how to remain an artist once he grows up.
Pablo Picasso

Modern art is like trying to follow the plot in alphabet soup.
Anonymous

The Arts (in general) *See also* Art & Artists; Books; Dancing; Movies; Music

You must have the Devil in you to succeed in any of the arts.
Voltaire

The purpose of art is the lifelong construction of a state of wonder.
Glenn Gould

All art requires courage.
Anne Tucker

Art is the only way to run away without leaving home.
Twyla Tharp

Art is love.
William Holman Hunt

Art is delayed echo.
George Santayana

Bathroom Issues *See* Bummer—Bathroom Issues

Bitching & Moaning

Bitching and moaning and complaining about this life, and yet, not wanting to give it up for anybody or anything.
Keith Urban

Instead of complaining that the rosebush is full of thorns, be happy that the thorn bush has roses.

Proverb

If you have time to whine and complain about something, then you have the time to do something about it.

Anthony D'Angelo

Complaining is silly. Either act or forget.

Stefan Sagmeister

I personally believe we developed language because of our deep inner need to complain.

Lily Tomlin

Books

"Book club" is code for "Drinking with the girls."

Anonymous

Always read something that will make you look good if you die in the middle of it.

P. J. O'Rourke

For people who like that kind of a book,
that is the kind of a book they will like.
Abraham Lincoln

The covers of this book are too far apart.
Ambrose Bierce

A house without books is like a room
without windows.
Heinrich Mann

I read part of it all the way through.
Samuel Goldwyn

This is not a novel to be tossed aside
lightly. It should be thrown with great
force.
Dorothy Parker

Having been unpopular in high school is
not just cause for book publication.
Fran Lebowitz

Big book, big bore.
Callimachus

If you believe everything you read, better
not read.
Japanese proverb

Where is human nature so weak as in the bookstore?

Henry Ward Beecher

Just the knowledge that a good book is awaiting one at the end of a long day makes that day happier.

Kathleen Norris

Booorrrring! (boring people, boring situations)

He's the kind of bore who's here today and here tomorrow.

Binnie Barnes

If you are doing all the talking, you are boring somebody.

Helen Gurley Brown

Somebody's boring me. I think it's me.

Dylan Thomas

The secret of being a bore is to tell everything.

Voltaire

He had nothing to say—and said
it endlessly.
Anonymous

A bore is a man who, when you ask him
how he is, tells you.
Bert Leston Taylor

Listen, or your tongue will keep you deaf.
Native American proverb

Nothing happens, nobody comes, nobody
goes. It's awful!
Samuel Beckett [in the play Waiting for
Godot*]*

Beam me up, Scotty.
William Shatner [in the TV program Star Trek*;
purists will note this phrase was never actually
said—instead, Shatner (Captain Kirk) would
actually intone "Beam us up, Mr. Scott."
Nevertheless, it's now the expected wording,
and it's useful when you're bored to death.]*

Bravery   See Courage

Bummer *See also* Problems. *See also whatever strikes you as a bummer:* Anger; Arguments & Fighting; Death & Dying; Divorce; *etc.*

Bad Dates

So many roads. So many detours. So many choices. So many mistakes.
Sarah Jessica Parker [in the TV show Sex and the City*]*

I can't go on any more bad dates. I would rather be home alone than out with some guy who sells socks on the internet.
Cynthia Nixon [in the TV program Sex and the City*]*

Bathroom Issues

Always go to the bathroom when you have a chance.
King George V

Why do they lock gas station bathrooms? Are they afraid someone will clean them?
Anonymous

Men who leave the toilet seat up secretly want women to get up to go to the bathroom in the middle of the night and fall in.

Rita Rudner

Always pee before a long car trip.

Martin Mull

Anything dropped in the bathroom falls in the toilet.

Anonymous

The length of a film should be directly related to the endurance of the human bladder.

Alfred Hitchcock

It is better to have a relationship with someone who cheats on you than with someone who does not flush the toilet.

Uma Thurman

Can you spare a square?

Julia Louis-Dreyfus [in the TV program Seinfeld]

Car Problems

The journey of a hundred miles begins with a broken fan belt and a flat tire.

Anonymous

Dental Stuff

We all basically go back to being a child when we're in a dentist's chair.

Arthur Benjamin

Happiness is your dentist telling you it won't hurt and then having him catch his hand in the drill.

Johnny Carson

Brush them & floss them & take them to the dentist, & they will stay with you. Ignore them, & they'll go away.

American Dental Association

Better a tooth out than always aching.

Thomas Fuller [a phrase that might apply to many situations!]

If suffering brought wisdom, the dentist's office would be full of luminous ideas.

Mason Cooley

Farts & Farting

My philosophy of dating is to just fart right away.

Jenny McCarthy

Women don't fart—we release tension.

Anonymous

Fired!

Nothing bad's going to happen to us. If we get fired, it's not failure; it's a midlife vocational reassessment.

P. J. O'Rourke

There's nothing wrong with being fired.

Ted Turner

Most people work just hard enough not to get fired and get paid just enough money not to quit.

George Carlin

Flying

If God had really intended men to fly, he'd make it easier to get to the airport.

George Winters

You define a good flight by negatives: you didn't get hijacked, you didn't crash, you didn't throw up, you weren't late.
Paul Theroux

There are two kinds of air travel in the United States: first class and third world.
Bobby Slayton

Airline travel is hours of boredom interrupted by moments of stark terror.
Al Boliska

The most dangerous thing about flying is the risk of starving to death.
Dick Depew

The scientific theory I like best is that the rings of Saturn are composed entirely of lost airline luggage.
Mike Russell

Airplane travel is nature's way of making you look like your passport photo.
Al Gore

Jet lag is for amateurs.
Dick Clark

Hangovers

He resolved, having done it once, never to move his eyeballs again.
Kingsley Amis

A real hangover is nothing to try family remedies on. The only cure for a real hangover is death.
Robert Benchley

His mouth had been used as a latrine by some small creature of the night and then as its mausoleum.
Kingsley Amis

Housecleaning

What a dump!
Bette Davis [in the movie Beyond the Forest]

[Is it] time to wash the dishes and clean your house? Look inside your pants. If you find a penis in there, it's not time.
Jo Brand

After the first four years the dirt doesn't get any worse.
Quentin Crisp

Housework won't kill you, but why take a chance?

Phyllis Diller

My idea of housework is to sweep the room with a glance.

Anonymous

Dirt will always win in the end.

Bob Rosenthal

Jury Duty

Ever notice how random chance always picks you for jury duty, but never to win the lottery?

Alfred E. Neuman [& Mad magazine editors]

Getting out of jury duty is easy. The trick is to say you're prejudiced against all races.

Homer Simpson [in the TV program The Simpsons]

Lawsuits

Avoid lawsuits beyond all things; they pervert your conscience, impair your health, and dissipate your property.

Jean de la Bruyere

Lawyers, I suppose, were children once.
Charles Lamb

Where there's a will, there's a lawsuit.
Voltaire

Lawsuit: A machine which you go into as a pig and come out of as sausage.
Ambrose Bierce

I was never ruined but twice: once when I lost a lawsuit and once when I won one.
Voltaire

Mosquitoes

Mosquitoes remind us that we are not as high up on the food chain as we think.
Tom Wilson

The mosquito is the state bird of New Jersey.
Andy Warhol

Parking

I like to drive downtown and get a great parking spot, then sit in my car and count how many people ask me if I'm leaving.
Steven Wright [on boredom]

Those who cannot remember the past will spend a lot of time looking for their cars in mall parking lots.

Jay Trachman

Periods/PMS

The curse has come upon me.... How did St. Joan manage? All that armor. How did Pavlova, when she danced *Swan Lake*?

Phyllida Law

I had no idea what a period was. When older girls said the word, I just thought they were talking about sentence structure.

Susan Shutan

Who invented tampons? Have they been knighted?

Phyllida Law

[PMS]...the only time of the month I can be myself.

Roseanne Barr

I don't have PMS—I'm just naturally bitchy!

Anonymous

Plumbing Problems

Not only is there no God, but try getting a plumber on weekends.

Woody Allen

Anybody who has any doubt about the ingenuity or the resourcefulness of a plumber never got a bill from one.

George Meany

The flush toilet is the basis of Western civilization.

Alan Coult

Seasickness

The only cure for seasickness is to sit on the shady side of an old brick church in the country.

English sailors' proverb

How saintly people look when seasick.

Samuel Butler

A man who wants to vomit never puts on airs.

Josh Billings

Taxes

Simplified tax form: How much money did you make last year? Mail it in.

Anonymous

People who complain about taxes can be divided into two classes: men and women.

Anonymous

Why does a slight tax increase cost you 200 dollars and a substantial tax cut save you 30 cents?

Peg Bracken

Bumper Stickers

Except where noted, all these phrases were created by the well-known and oft-quoted Anonymous.

About Bumper Stickers

There's a difference between a philosophy and a bumper sticker.

Charles M. Schulz

Great Bumper Stickers

Think globally, act locally.

Non-Judgment Day is near.

Size does matter.

Why do psychics have to ask for your name?

Using your turn signal is not giving secret information to the enemy.

Biodiesel. Praise the Lard!

Back off! I'm not that kind of car.

Calmness

Keep calm and carry on.
British government wartime poster

But I can't function when I'm calm!
Ashleigh Brilliant

Nothing is so aggravating as calmness.
Oscar Wilde

Be like a duck. Calm on the surface, but always paddling like the dickens underneath.

Michael Caine

After a storm comes a calm.

Anonymous

Cars See Driving & Traffic; *see also* Bummer—Car Problems

Cats See Animals

Cell Phones

Watching something on your cell phone seems like crazy talk to me.

Matt Thompson

Apparently we love our own cell phones but we hate everyone else's.

Joe Bob Briggs

Cell phones are the latest invention in rudeness.

Terri Guillemets

1 in 10 [survey respondents] said they'd rather lose their mother-in-law than their cell phone.
Léger Marketing

Mobile phones are the only subject on which men boast about who's got the smallest.
Neil Kinnock

Chance See Risk & Chance

Change

People change and forget to tell each other.
Lillian Hellman

Change is just the way things are.
Buddha

Nothing endures but change.
Heraclitus

Do not feel certain of anything.
Bertrand Russell

To go forward, one must often reverse one's position.

Anonymous

There is nothing wrong with change, if it's in the right direction.

Winston Churchill

Change is inevitable—except from a vending machine.

Robert C. Gallagher

When you're finished changing, you're finished.

Benjamin Franklin

Insanity is doing the same thing over and over again, but expecting different results.

Albert Einstein [among others, including Rita Mae Brown]

She must have change, she must!

William Shakespeare

The most powerful agent of change is a change of heart.

B. J. Marshall

Everything flows, nothing stands still.
Hereclitus

Children

The Good

A baby is God's opinion that life should
go on.
Carl Sandburg

Babies are such a nice way to start people.
Don Herold

Children are the living messages we send
to a time we will not see.
John W. Whitehead

Truly wonderful the mind of a child is.
Yoda [in the movie Star Wars: Attack of the
Clones]

Children reinvent your world for you.
Susan Sarandon

The Bad

A two-year-old is kind of like having a blender, but you don't have a top for it.

Jerry Seinfeld

Having a baby is like getting the world's worst roommate, like having Janis Joplin with a bad hangover and PMS come to stay.

Anne Lamott

All children are essentially criminal.

Denis Diderot

Do not allow your children to mix drinks. It is unseemly and they use too much vermouth.

Fran Lebowitz

A child is a curly, dimpled lunatic.

Ralph Waldo Emerson

The thing about having a baby is that thereafter you have it.

Jean Kerr

Pregnancy

Don't make a baby if you can't be a father.

National Urban League slogan

If pregnancy were a book, they would cut the last two chapters.
Meryl Streep [in the movie Heartburn*]*

To me, life is tough enough without having someone kick you from the inside.
Rita Rudner

Childbirth

Giving birth is like taking your lower lip and forcing it over your head.
Carol Burnett

I don't know nuthin' 'bout birthin' no babies!
Butterfly McQueen [in the movie Gone with the Wind*]*

Babies

I can't think why mothers love them. All babies do is leak at both ends.
William Faulkner

Diaper backwards spells repaid. Think about it.
Marshall McLuhan

A loud noise at one end and no sense of responsibility at the other.

Ronald Knox

People who say they sleep like a baby usually don't have one.

L. J. Burke

Childhood

No one has a normal childhood.

Laura Chester

Everything else you grow out of, but you never recover from childhood.

Beryl Bainbridge

Children's talent to endure stems from their ignorance of alternatives.

Maya Angelou

Children need love, especially when they do not deserve it.

Harold S. Hulbert

Who knows the thoughts of a child?

Nora Perry

If you carry your childhood with you, you never become older.

Tom Stoppard

There is always one moment in childhood when the door opens and lets the future in.

Graham Greene

Little girls are cute and small only to adults. To one another they are not cute. They are life-sized.

Margaret Atwood

Children should neither be seen nor heard from—ever again.

W. C. Fields

Teenagers

You know that children are growing up when they start asking questions that have answers.

John J. Plomp

Never lend your car to anyone to whom you've given birth.

Erma Bombeck

Telling a teenager the facts of life is like giving a fish a bath.
Arnold Glasgow

Adolescents turn on you—that's their job.
Ron Howard

Adolescence is just one big walking pimple.
Carol Burnett

Parents & Parenthood

[My mother] could stop you from doing anything....Without saying a word, she has that power to rip out your tonsils.
Whoopi Goldberg

They fuck you up, your mum and dad....
Philip Larkin

Trust yourself. You know more than you think you do.
Benjamin Spock

Raising kids is part joy and part guerrilla warfare.
Ed Asner

The law of heredity is that all undesirable traits come from the other parent.

Anonymous

Whatever else is unsure in this stinking dunghill of a world, a mother's love is not.

James Joyce

No matter how old a mother is, she watches her middle-aged children for signs of improvement.

Florida Scott-Maxwell

The toughest part of parenthood is never knowing if you're doing the right thing.

D. L. Stewart

You can learn many things from children. How much patience you have, for instance.

Franklin P. Jones

The time not to become a father is 18 years before a war.

E. B. White

It is easy to become a father, but very difficult to be a father.

William Busch

Children need models rather than critics.

Joseph Joubert

Clothes & Fashion

When in doubt, wear red.

Bill Blass

She wears her clothes as if they were thrown on with a pitchfork.

Jonathan Swift

I base my fashion taste on what doesn't itch.

Gilda Radner

You'd be surprised how much it costs to look this cheap.

Dolly Parton

Neckties strangle clear thinking.

Lin Yutang

You can be better dressed when you own a lot of stuff.

Helen Gurley Brown

You mean those clothes of hers are intentional?

Dorothy Parker

The only thing that separates us from the animals is our ability to accessorize.

Olympia Dukakis [in the movie Steel Magnolias*]*

One-third of your life is spent in bed, two-thirds of your life in clothes.

E. L. Brentlinger

I say dress up every day; you never know when you're going to meet your next husband.

Laura Bennett

Beware of any enterprise that requires new clothes.

Henry David Thoreau

She looks like she was poured into that dress and forgot to say when.

Anonymous

You should never have your best trousers on when you go out to fight for freedom and truth.

Henrik Ibsen

No one in the world needs a mink coat but a mink.

Anonymous

It is totally impossible to be well dressed in cheap clothes.

Hardy Amies

Men who wear turtlenecks look like turtles.

Doris Lilly

Fashion is what one wears oneself. What is unfashionable is what other people wear.

Oscar Wilde

A wacky, trendy outfit on a guy over 40 indicates he's got big issues.

Merrill Markoe

Nothing goes right if your underwear's tight.

Hanes advertisement

Clutter   *See also* Simplicity

Anyone can buy new things, but only a strong man can throw out old things.
William Feather

Everything you buy is an added burden.
Billy Ocean

You can't have everything. Where would you put it?
Steven Wright

If you don't enjoy what you already have, how could you be happier with more?
Anonymous

Complaining   *See* Bitching & Moaning

Computers   *See also* Internet

I'm sorry, Dave. I can't do that.
HAL 9000 [in the movie 2001: A Space Odyssey]

Never trust a computer you can't throw out of a window.
Steve Wozniak

The computer is down. I hope it's something serious.

Stanton Delaplane

A computer once beat me at chess, but it was no match for me at kickboxing.

Emo Philips

Don't anthropomorphize computers. They don't like it.

Anonymous

The computer is a moron.

Peter Drucker

The real danger is not that computers will begin to think like men, but that men will begin to think like computers.

Sydney J. Harris

What do people mean when they say the computer went down on them?

Marilyn Pittman

That's not a bug, that's a feature.

Anonymous

I am not the only person who uses his computer mainly for the purpose of diddling with his computer.

Dave Barry

Treat your password like your toothbrush. Don't let anybody else use it, and get a new one every six months.

Clifford Stoll

Back up my hard drive? How do I put it in reverse?

Anonymous

Hardware: the parts of a computer that can be kicked.

Jeff Pesis

Where is the "any" key?

Homer Simpson [in response to the message "Press any key"; in the TV program The Simpsons]

Why is it drug addicts and computer aficionados are both called users?

Clifford Stoll

Consistency

Consistency is contrary to nature, contrary to life. The only completely consistent people are the dead.

Aldous Huxley

A foolish consistency is the hobgoblin of little minds....

Ralph Waldo Emerson

Consistency is the last refuge of the unimaginative.

Oscar Wilde

Cooks & Cooking

Life is too short to stuff a mushroom.

Shirley Conran

Cooking is like love. It should be entered into with abandon or not at all.

Harriet Van Horne

Even an old boot tastes good if it's cooked over charcoal.

Italian proverb

It's so beautifully arranged on the plate—
you know someone's fingers have been all
over it.
Julia Child

I don't even butter my bread. I consider
that cooking.
Katherine Cebrian

The French cook; we open tins.
John Galsworthy

I was 32 when I started cooking; up until
then, I just ate.
Julia Child

In the childhood memories of every good
cook, there's a large kitchen, a warm stove,
a simmering pot, and a mom.
Barbara Costikyan

If you can organize your kitchen, you can
organize your life.
Louis Parrish

Who bothers to cook TV dinners? I suck
them frozen.
Woody Allen

Always remember: If you're alone in the kitchen and you drop the lamb, you can always just pick it up. Who's going to know?

Julia Child

I no longer prepare food or drink with more than one ingredient.

Cyra McFadden

Courage *See also* Fear

You're braver than you believe, and stronger than you seem, and smarter than you think.

Christopher Robin to Pooh [A. A. Milne]

The best way out is always through.

Robert Frost

This is no time for ease and comfort. It is time to dare and endure.

Winston Churchill

Have the courage to live. Anyone can die.

Robert Cody

Courage is the art of being the only one who knows you're scared to death.
Harold Wilson

Courage is resistance to fear, mastery of fear, not absence of fear.
Mark Twain

Creativity & Inspiration

The secret to creativity is knowing how to hide your sources.
Albert Einstein

Creativity comes from trust. Trust your instincts. And never hope more than you work.
Rita Mae Brown

Desperation is sometimes as powerful an inspirer as genius.
Benjamin Disraeli

The chief enemy of creativity is "good" sense.
Pablo Picasso

Think sideways!

Edward de Bono

The best way to have a good idea is to have lots of ideas.

Linus Pauling

Creativity requires the courage to let go of certainties.

Erich Fromm

You can't wait for inspiration; you have to go after it with a club.

Jack London

All great deeds and all great thoughts have a ridiculous beginning.

Albert Camus

Ideas are like rabbits. You get a couple and learn how to handle them, and pretty soon you have a dozen.

John Steinbeck

I can't understand why people are frightened of new ideas. I'm frightened of the old ones.

John Cage

Ideas come from space.
Thomas Edison

Trust that small still voice that says, "This might work and I'll try it."
Diane Mariechild

Listen to the voices.
William Faulkner

I do my best work when I'm in pain and turmoil.
Sting

Culture   See Art & Artists; The Arts (in general); Books; Dancing; Movies; Music

Dancing

Life may not be the party we hoped for—but while we're here, we should dance.
Anonymous

The one thing that can solve most of our problems is dancing.
James Brown

I love dancing. I think it's better to dance than to march through life.
Yoko Ono

You and I are past our dancing days.
William Shakespeare

Every day we must dance, if only in our thoughts.
Rebbe Nachman of Breslov

No sane man will dance.
Cicero

Will you, won't you, will you, won't you, will you join the dance?
Lewis Carroll

I would believe only in a God that knows how to dance.
Friedrich Nietzsche

We're fools whether we dance or not, so we might as well dance.
Japanese proverb

Nobody cares if you can't dance well. Just get up and dance.
Dave Barry

Dance till the stars come down from the rafters, dance, dance, dance till you drop.
W. H. Auden

Dance first. Think later. It's the natural order.
Samuel Beckett

Do you think dyslexic people have difficulty dancing to "Y.M.C.A."?
Dave Sokolowsk

Never trust spiritual leader who cannot dance.
Pat Morita [in the movie The Next Karate Kid*]*

Dance, even if you have nowhere to do it but your living room.
Kurt Vonnegut

If I can't dance, I don't want to be part of your revolution.
Emma Goldman

We should consider every day lost in which we don't dance.
Friedrich Nietzsche

God respects you when you work, but he loves you when you dance.

Sufi saying

God match me with a good dancer.

William Shakespeare

If you can walk, you can dance. If you can talk, you can sing.

Zimbabwean proverb

Death & Dying

Everybody dies.

John Garfield

Death is nature's way of telling you to slow down.

Anonymous

Any man who says he is not afraid of death is a liar.

Winston Churchill

I do not approve of mourning; I approve only of remembering.

Noël Coward

Death is like the rumble of distant thunder at a picnic.
W. H. Auden

Everybody has to die, but I've always believed an exception would be made in my case.
William Saroyan

I don't want to achieve immortality through my work...I want to achieve it through not dying.
Woody Allen

I believe in reincarnation, so I've left all my money to myself.
Tony Blackburn

Everything passes, everything wears out, everything breaks.
French proverb

In this world nothing can be said to be certain, except death and taxes.
Benjamin Franklin

Death and taxes and childbirth! There's never any convenient time for any of them.
Margaret Mitchell [in the book Gone with the Wind]

One dies only once and it's for such a long time!
Molière

Death is nature's way of saying "Howdy."
Anonymous

When you cease to make a contribution, you begin to die.
Eleanor Roosevelt

To die will be an awfully big adventure.
J. M. Barrie [in the play Peter Pan]

Dentists See Bummer—Dental Stuff

Determination & Persistence

Fall seven times, stand up eight.
Japanese proverb

Those who don't do anything never make mistakes.
Théodore de Banville

If you don't crack the shell, you can't eat the nut.
Persian proverb

The shortest answer is doing.
George Herbert

Do or do not do. There is no try.
Yoda [in the movie Star Wars: The Empire Strikes Back]

Just do it.
Nike

Never, never, never, never…give in, except to convictions of honor and good sense.
Winston Churchill

The little engine kept bravely puffing faster and faster, "I think I can, I think I can, I think I can."
Watty Piper [in the book The Little Engine That Could]

He who limps still walks.

Stanislaw Lec

If at first you don't succeed, get a bigger hammer.

Alan Lewis

When you get to the end of your rope, tie a knot and hang on.

Franklin D. Roosevelt

Little by little, one walks far.

Peruvian proverb

After all, computers crash, people die, relationships fall apart. The best we can do is breathe and reboot.

Sarah Jessica Parker [in the TV program Sex and the City]

Diets & Dieting See also Food; Meals

[She thinks] you don't get fat if no one sees you eating.

Gloria Naylor

Probably nothing in the world arouses more false hopes than the first four hours of a diet.

Dan Bennett

I've been on a diet for two weeks and all I've lost is two weeks.

Totie Fields

[She's] a light eater. As soon as it's light, she starts eating.

Henny Youngman

"How long does getting thin take?" asked Pooh anxiously.

A. A. Milne [in Winnie the Pooh*]*

Never eat more than you can lift.

Miss Piggy

I'm not overweight. I'm just nine inches too short.

Shelley Winters

The only time to eat diet food is while you're waiting for the steak to cook.

Julia Child

Please sir, I want some more.
Charles Dickens [in the book Oliver Twist*]*

The second day of a diet is always easier than the first. By the second day you're off it.
Jackie Gleason

If one eats less, one will taste more.
Chinese proverb

Avoid any diet that discourages the use of hot fudge.
Don Kardong

I have a great diet. You're allowed to eat anything you want, but you must eat it with naked fat people.
Ed Bluestone

Digestion & Indigestion

Eat what you like and let the food fight it out inside.
Mark Twain

All I ask of food is that it doesn't harm me.
Michael Palin [of Monty Python]

If you don't chew your food, who will?

Anonymous

Don't tell your friends about your indigestion: "How are you!" is a greeting, not a question.

Arthur Guiterman

Dining Out See *also* Entertaining

You are where you eat.

Pamela Fiori

One cannot think well, love well, sleep well, if one has not dined well.

Virginia Woolf

I don't care where I sit as long as I get fed.

Calvin Trillin

Nouvelle cuisine, roughly translated, means: I can't believe I paid 96 dollars and I'm still hungry.

Mike Kalin

"Escargot" is French for "fat crawling bag of phlegm."

Dave Barry

The disparity between a restaurant's price and food quality rises in direct proportion to the size of the pepper mill.

Bryan Miller

Divorce

A wife lasts for the length of the marriage, but an ex-wife is there *for the rest of your life.*

Jim Samuels

It's relaxing to go out with my ex-wife because she already knows I'm an idiot.

Warren Thomas

The happiest time of anyone's life is just after the first divorce.

John Kenneth Galbraith

Ah, yes…divorce… from the Latin word meaning "to rip out a man's genitals through his wallet."

Robin Williams

A divorce is like an amputation: You survive, but there's less of you.

Margaret Atwood

Just another of our many disagreements. He wants a no-fault divorce, whereas I would prefer to have the bastard crucified.

J. B. Handlesman

You never really know a man until you have divorced him.

Zsa Zsa Gabor

My mother always said, "Don't marry for money, divorce for money."

Wendy Liebman

Marriage is the chief cause of divorce.

Groucho Marx

I don't think I'll get married again; I'll just find a woman I don't like and give her a house.

Lewis Grizzard

I've never been married, but I tell people I'm divorced so they won't think something's wrong with me.

Elayne Boosler

Dogs *See* Animals

Dreams & Wishes *See also* Sleep & Sleeping—Dreaming

If your dreams turn to dust...vacuum.
Anonymous

Nothing happens unless first a dream.
Carl Sandburg

Those who abandon their dreams will discourage yours.
Anonymous

Keep your eyes on the stars and your feet on the ground.
Theodore Roosevelt

When you cease to dream, you cease to live.
Malcolm Forbes

Vision is the art of seeing things invisible.
Jonathan Swift

Go for it.
Anonymous

Drinks & Drinking   **See also** Bummer—
Hangovers

Alcoholic

A meal without wine is breakfast.

Anonymous

There comes a time in every woman's life
when the only thing that helps is a glass of
champagne.

Bette Davis [in the movie Old Acquaintance*]*

Only Irish coffee provides in a single glass
all four essential food groups: alcohol,
caffeine, sugar, and fat.

Alex Levine

People who drink to drown their sorrow
should be told that sorrow knows how to
swim.

Ann Landers

What contemptible scoundrel stole the
cork from my lunch?

W. C. Fields

I rather like bad wine...one gets so bored
with good wine.

Benjamin Disraeli

The problem with the world is that everyone is a few drinks behind.
Humphrey Bogart

An alcoholic is someone you don't like who drinks as much as you do.
Dylan Thomas

Nothing anyone says in a bar is true.
Mark Ruffalo

Wine is bottled poetry.
Robert Louis Stevenson

Champagne! I love it. It tastes like your foot is asleep.
Joan Davis [in the movie George White's Scandals*]*

Wine is proof that God loves us and wants us to be happy.
Anonymous [This is often attributed to Benjamin Franklin, and sometimes "beer" is substituted for "wine."]

One reason I don't drink is that I want to know when I'm having a good time.
Nancy Astor

My only regret in life is that I did not drink more champagne.

John Maynard Keynes

I drink to keep body and soul apart.

Oscar Wilde

I've made it a rule never to drink by daylight and never to refuse a drink after dark.

H. L. Mencken

'Tis not the drinking that is to be blamed, but the excess.

John Selden

Alcohol may not solve your problems, but neither will water or milk.

Anonymous

Nonalcoholic

Coffee should be black as hell, strong as death, and sweet as love.

Proverb

If I can't drink my bowl of coffee three times a day, then in my torment I will shrivel like a piece of roast goat.

J. S. Bach [in his Coffee Cantata*]*

Ever wonder about those people who spend $2 apiece on those little bottles of Evian water? Try spelling Evian backward.

George Carlin

Water is the only drink for a wise man.

Henry David Thoreau

Water, taken in moderation, cannot hurt anybody.

Mark Twain

There is no trouble so great or grave that cannot be much diminished by a nice cup of tea.

Bernard-Paul Heroux

While there's tea, there's hope.

Arthur Wing Pinero

Driving & Traffic *See also* Bummer—Parking

Cab drivers are living proof that practice does not make perfect.

Howard Ogden

Why do they call it rush hour when nothing moves?

Robin Williams

Traffic is like a bad dog. It isn't important to look both ways when crossing the street. It's important to not show fear.

P. J. O'Rourke

Traffic signals in New York are just rough guidelines.

David Letterman

You don't watch for potholes around here, you watch for the little roadway between them.

Raza Manji

Have you ever noticed? Anybody going slower than you is an idiot, and anyone going faster than you is a maniac.

George Carlin

You never really learn to swear until you learn to drive.

Anonymous

Drugs

Don't do speed. Speed turns you into your parents.

Frank Zappa

When I was a kid I inhaled frequently. That was the point.

Barack Obama

I say no to drugs. But they won't listen.

Anonymous

Long-term peace—except maybe "rest in peace"—is not found in a chemical. Being half-conscious always slaps back.

Grace Slick

Cocaine is God's way of saying you're making too much money.

Robin Williams

Dope will get you through times of no money better than money will get you through times of no dope.
Gilbert Shelton

The most deadly thing about cocaine is that it separates you from your soul.
Quincy Jones

I knew who I *was* when I got up this morning, but I must have been changed several times since then.
Alice [in Lewis Carroll's book Alice in Wonderland*]*

I wouldn't recommend sex, drugs, or insanity for everyone, but they've always worked for me.
Hunter Thompson

Dumb...Dumber...Dumbest

Except where noted, all these phrases were created by the well-known and oft-quoted Anonymous.

You aren't too bright. I like that in a man.
Kathleen Turner [in the movie Body Heat*]*

Your ignorance cramps my conversation.
Anthony Hope

His mind is so open that the wind whistles through it.
Heywood Broun

Any dumber he'd be a begonia.
Molly Ivins

Strong as an ox, with the brains of a tractor.
Edna Buchanan

He's as dumb as a salad bar.
Garrison Keillor

He's not flying on all thrusters.
Mr. Spock [in the TV program Star Trek*]*

He's half a bubble off plumb.

She's two bees short of a hive.

Sad. The good Lord only gave her first gear.

I can see the wheel spinning, but the hamster is dead.

He's a taco short of a combination box.

Her intellect is rivaled only by garden tools.

She comes from a shallow gene pool.

His tray table is not in its fully upright and locked position.

Dumber than a bag of hammers.

If you stand close enough to him, you can hear the ocean.

Dying See Death & Dying

Eating See Cooks & Cooking; Diets & Dieting; Digestion & Indigestion; Food; Meals; Vegetarians & Vegetarianism

Education

It's a miracle that curiosity survives formal education.

Albert Einstein

In real life, I assure you, there is no such thing as algebra.

Fran Lebowitz

I have never let my schooling interfere with my education.
Mark Twain

Experience is a good school, but the fees are high.
Heinrich Heine

Those who have the privilege to know, have the duty to act.
Albert Einstein

We don't know a millionth of one percent about anything.
Thomas A. Edison

Much learning doth make thee mad.
Bible

If you can't explain your ideas to your grandmother in terms she understands, you don't know your subject well enough.
Matthew Frederick`

Everybody is ignorant, only on different subjects.
Will Rogers

I think the world is run by C students.

Anonymous

Some people drink from the fountain of knowledge; others just gargle.

Robert Anthony

Enemies See Friends & Enemies

Entertaining

Parties (dinner parties, cocktail parties, party parties)

For a single woman, preparing for company means wiping the lipstick off the milk carton.

Elayne Boosler

Support wildlife. Throw a party.

Anonymous

It isn't so much what's on the table that matters, as what's on the chairs.

W. S. Gilbert

Unless your life is going well, you don't dream of giving a party.
Carol Shields

The art of being a good guest is knowing when to leave.
Duke of Edinburgh

Some people stay longer in an hour than others do in a month.
William Dean Howells

There's somebody at every dinner party who eats all the celery.
Kin Hubbard

I'm looking for a party where I can be the designated eater.
Ashleigh Brilliant

Society is no comfort to one not sociable.
William Shakespeare

The dying process begins the minute we are born, but it accelerates during dinner parties.
Carol Matthau

At a dinner party, one should eat wisely but not too well, and talk well but not too wisely.

W. Somerset Maugham

Lately it has become more and more difficult to attend dinner parties without the evening ending in gunfire or tapioca.

Daniel Handler

Houseguests & Visitors

Houseguests and fish smell on the third day.

Anonymous

The only way to entertain some folks is to listen to them.

Kin Hubbard

Superior people never make long visits.

Marianne Moore

May our house always be too small to hold all our friends.

Myrtle Reed

It was a delightful visit; perfect, in being much too short.
Virginia Woolf

Etiquette

Etiquette is knowing how to yawn with your mouth closed.
Herbert V. Prochnow

Etiquette tip: More people will get out of your way if you say "I'm gonna puke!" than if you say "Excuse me."
Anonymous

I prefer the Chinese method of eating.... You can do anything at the dining table except arm wrestle.
Jeff Smith

The world was my oyster but I used the wrong fork.
Oscar Wilde

Good breeding consists in concealing how much we think of ourselves and how little we think of the other person.
Mark Twain

Rudeness is the weak man's imitation of strength.

Eric Hoffer

Etiquette is what you are doing when people are looking and listening. What you are thinking is your business.

Virginia Cary Hudson

Evenings See Sleep & Sleeping—Evenings

Exercise

Muscles come and go; flab lasts.

William E. Vaughan

Exercise is the yuppie version of bulimia.

Barbara Ehrenreich

I am pushing sixty. That is enough exercise for me.

Mark Twain

I really don't think I need buns of steel. I'd be happy with buns of cinnamon.

Ellen DeGeneres

Bodies never lie.
Agnes De Mille

If you don't make time for exercise now, make time for illness later.
Anonymous

Avoid running at all times.
Satchel Paige

A man's health can be judged by which he takes two at a time—pills or stairs.
Joan Welsh

I have to exercise in the morning before my brain figures out what I'm doing.
Marsha Doble

An hour of basketball feels like 15 minutes. An hour on a treadmill feels like a weekend in traffic school.
David Walters

I consider exercise vulgar. It makes people smell.
Alec Yuill-Thornton

If your dog is fat, you're not getting enough exercise.
Anonymous

Physical fitness can neither be achieved by wishful thinking nor outright purchase.
Joseph Pilates

I believe that every human has a finite number of heartbeats. I don't intend to waste any of mine running around doing exercises.
Buzz Aldrin

Walking isn't a lost art: one must, by some means, get to the garage.
Evan Esar

Failure See Success & Failure

Family See also Children

Big sisters are the crabgrass in the lawn of life.
Charles M. Schulz

I am an only child. I have one sister.
Woody Allen

Happiness is having a large, loving, caring, close-knit family in another city.
George Burns

Other things may change us, but we start and end with the family.
Anthony Brandt

There is no such thing as fun for the whole family.
Jerry Seinfeld

Call it a clan, call it a network, call it a tribe, call it a family. Whatever you call it, whoever you are, you need one.
Jane Howard

Families are about love overcoming emotional torture.
Matt Groening

Family faces are magic mirrors. Looking at people who belong to us, we see the past, present, and future.
Gail Lumet Buckley

Friends are God's apology for relations.
Hugh Kingsmill

The great advantage of living in a large family is that early lesson of life's essential unfairness.
Nancy Mitford

Nobody's family can hang out the sign,
"Nothing the matter here."
Chinese proverb

Farewells

I hate goodbye. I know what I need. I need
more hellos.
Charles M. Schulz [in the comic strip Peanuts]

A goodbye isn't painful unless you're never
going to say hello again.
Anonymous

Be well, do good work, and keep in touch.
Garrison Keillor

Why does it take a minute to say hello and
forever to say goodbye?
Anonymous

Exit, pursued by a bear.
William Shakespeare [stage direction]

Farts & Farting   See Bummer—Farts & Farting

Fashion See Clothes & Fashion

Fear See also Courage

Fear is not an unknown emotion to us.
Neil Armstrong

To him who is in fear, everything rustles.
Sophocles

Man cannot live by dread alone.
Anonymous

The first and great commandment is, Don't let them scare you.
Elmer Davis

Always do what you are afraid to do.
Ralph Waldo Emerson

Fear is static that prevents me from hearing myself.
Samuel Butler

All forms of fear produce fatigue.
Bertrand Russell

Fear is the path to the Dark Side. Fear leads to anger, anger leads to hate, hate leads to suffering.
Yoda [in the movie Star Wars: The Phantom Menace*]*

Fighting *See Arguments & Fighting*

Flatulence *See Bummer—Farts & Farting*

Flying *See Bummer—Flying*

Food *See also Cooks & Cooking; Diets & Dieting; Meals; Vegetarians & Vegetarianism*

Eat to live, and not live to eat.
Benjamin Franklin

There is no such thing as a little garlic.
Arthur Baer

Never eat anything you can't pronounce.
Erma Bombeck

Food is an important part of a balanced diet.
Fran Lebowitz

The first time I ate organic whole-grain bread I swear it tasted like roofing material.

Robin Williams

My idea of feng shui is to have them arrange the pepperoni in a circle on my pizza.

Anonymous

Man cannot live by bread alone; he must have peanut butter.

James A. Garfield

I'm still looking for a man who could excite me as much as a baked potato.

Laura Flynn McCarthy

The trouble with eating Italian food is that five or six days later you're hungry again.

George Miller

It is hard to imagine a civilization without onions.

Julia Child

There is no such thing as a pretty good omelet.

French proverb

The most dangerous food is wedding cake.
American proverb

Health food makes me sick.
Calvin Trillin

[Cheese is] milk's leap toward immortality.
Clifton Fadiman

I will not eat oysters. I want my food dead.
Not sick, not wounded, dead.
Woody Allen

Everything you see I owe to spaghetti.
Sophia Loren

Me want cookie.
Cookie Monster [in the TV program Sesame
Street]

He was a bold man that first ate an oyster.
Jonathan Swift

Peanut butter is the pâté of childhood.
Florence Fabricant

As for butter versus margarine, I trust cows
more than chemists.
Joan Gussow

Eating an artichoke is like getting to know someone really well.
Willi Hastings

Sex is good, but not as good as fresh sweet corn.
Garrison Keillor

I also avoid green vegetables. They're grossly overrated.
Noël Coward

Without ice cream, there would be darkness and chaos.
Don Kardong

Forgetfulness See Memory & Memories

Forgiveness

It's easier to ask forgiveness than it is to get permission.
Grace Hopper

Love truth, but pardon error.
Voltaire

Without forgiveness, there's no future.
Desmond Tutu

I have forgiven and forgotten all.
William Shakespeare

Always forgive your enemies; nothing annoys them so much.
Oscar Wilde

Of course he [God] will forgive me; that's his business.
Heinrich Heine [use Heine's original French (on his deathbed, no less) if so inclined: Bien sûr, il me pardonnera; c'est son métier.]

Forgiveness is the act of admitting we are like other people.
Christine Baldwin

The weak can never forgive. Forgiveness is the attribute of the strong.
Gandhi

Most of us can forgive and forget; we just don't want the other person to forget that we forgave.
Ivern Ball

If you can't forgive and forget, pick one.

Robert Brault

Forgiveness is the economy of the heart...
it saves the expense of anger, the cost of
hatred, the waste of spirits.

Hannah More

There's no point in burying the hatchet if
you're going to put up a marker on the
site.

Sydney J. Harris

Friends & Enemies

Friends

It is the friends you can call up at 4 a.m.
that matter.

Marlene Dietrich

However rare true love is, true friendship is
even rarer.

La Rochefoucauld

You'll always be my best friend. You know
too much.

Anonymous

Only your real friends will tell you when your face is dirty.
Sicilian proverb

A friend is one who dislikes the same people that you dislike.
Anonymous

All for one, one for all.
Alexandre Dumas [in the book The Three Musketeers; *classier:* Tous pour un, un pour tous.]

It is well, when judging a friend, to remember that he is judging you with the same godlike and superior impartiality.
Arnold Bennett

True friendship comes when silence between two people is comfortable.
Dave Tyson Gentry

It is one of the blessings of old friends that you afford to be stupid with them.
Ralph Waldo Emerson

The best mirror is an old friend.
English proverb

Friendship is born at that moment when one person says to another, "What! You too? I thought I was the only one."

C. S. Lewis

Enemies

Nobody ever forgets where he buried the hatchet.

Kin Hubbard

Love your enemies just in case your friends turn out to be a bunch of bastards.

R. A. Dickson

Even a paranoid can have enemies.

Henry Kissinger

Don't let your enemies dwell rent free in your head.

Barry Humphries [aka Dame Edna Everage]

Enemies are so stimulating.

Katharine Hepburn

A man cannot be too careful in the choice of his enemies.

Oscar Wilde

Frustration

There are times when one would like to hang the whole human race, and finish the farce.
Mark Twain

Set the kitchen timer for 20 minutes, cry, rant, rave, & at the sound of the bell, simmer down & go about business as usual.
Phyllis Diller

Future   See also Past

The day after tomorrow is the third day of the rest of your life.
George Carlin

The future is much like the present, only longer.
Don Quisenberry

The future just happened.
Michael Lewis

We are tomorrow's past.
Mary Webb

I never think of the future. It comes soon enough.
Albert Einstein

The best thing about the future is that it comes only one day at a time.
Abraham Lincoln

There is no data on the future.
Laurel Cutler

Cheer up! The worst is yet to come!
Philander Chase Johnson

Gay...So Very Gay

The state has no business in the bedrooms of the nation.
Pierre Trudeau

It always seemed to me a bit pointless to disapprove of homosexuality. It's like disapproving of rain.
Francis Maude

Labels are for filing. Labels are for clothing. Labels are not for people.
Martina Navratilova

It doesn't matter what you do, as long as you don't do it in public and frighten the horses.
Mrs. Patrick Campbell

The Lord is my Shepherd and he knows I'm gay.
Troy Perry

Be who you are and say what you feel, because those who mind don't matter and those who matter don't mind.
Dr. Seuss

Gaydar never lies.
[on the TV program The Larry Sanders Show]

Gossip

He who sows thorns should not go barefoot.
Proverb

I hate to spread rumors, but what else can one do with them?
Amanda Lear

People will believe anything if you whisper it.

Anonymous

It is awfully important to know what is and what is not your business.

Gertrude Stein

A lot of the troubles in the world would disappear if we were talking to each other instead of about each other.

Ronald Reagan

No one gossips about other people's secret virtues.

Bertrand Russell

If you haven't got anything nice to say about anybody, come sit next to me.

Alice Roosevelt Longworth

Gossip is when you hear something you like about someone you don't.

Earl Wilson

What you don't see with your eyes, don't invent with your tongue.

Jewish saying

Gratitude

I can no other answer make but thanks,
and thanks, and ever thanks.
William Shakespeare

Gratitude is the memory of the heart.
J. B. Massieu

Silent gratitude isn't much use to anyone.
G. B. Stern

I feel a very unusual sensation—if it is not
indigestion, I think it must be gratitude.
Benjamin Disraeli

I want to thank everybody who made this
day necessary.
Yogi Berra

Guilt

Guilt is the gift that keeps on giving.
Erma Bombeck

I don't know any woman who doesn't feel guilty about something. That's the guilt gene, right?
Hillary Clinton

He who knows no guilt knows no fear.
Philip Massinger

Everyone constructs his own bed of nails.
D. Sutten

The lady doth protest too much, methinks.
William Shakespeare

I'm an Irish Catholic and I have a long iceberg of guilt.
Edna O'Brien

Hangovers See Bummer—Hangovers

Happiness & Joy

A joy that's shared is a joy made double.
John Ray

The door to happiness opens outward.
Søren Kierkegaard

For peace of mind, resign as general manager of the universe.
Larry Eisenberg

Happiness is a direction, not a place.
Anonymous

Happiness is not a goal—it is a byproduct.
Eleanor Roosevelt

People are just about as happy as they make up their minds to be.
Abraham Lincoln

Joy is not in things; it is in us.
Richard Wagner

You have to sniff out joy, keep your nose to the joy-trail.
Buffy Sainte-Marie

If only we'd stop trying to be happy, we'd have a pretty good time.
Edith Wharton

Grief can take care of itself, but to get the full value of a joy you must have someone to divide it with.
Mark Twain

Happiness is nothing more than good
health and a bad memory.

Albert Schweitzer

Health See *also* Digestion & Indigestion

Never go to a doctor whose office plants
have died.

Erma Bombeck

My sore-throats, you know, are always
worse than anybody's.

Jane Austen [in the book Persuasion*]*

The cure for anything is salt water—sweat,
tears, or the sea.

Isak Dinesen

Always laugh when you can. It is cheap
medicine.

Lord Byron

Except for an occasional heart attack, I feel
as young as I ever did.

Robert Benchley

To do nothing is sometimes a good remedy.
Hippocrates

A hospital is no place to be sick.
Sam Goldwyn

People with bad coughs should go to doctors instead of theaters.
Alfred E. Neuman [& Mad magazine editors]

The kind of doctor I want is one who, when he's not examining me, is home studying medicine.
George S. Kaufman

I'm not unwell. I'm fucking dying.
Jeffrey Bernard

Hobbies

No gear, no hobby.
Anonymous

My personal hobbies are reading, listening to music, and silence.
Edith Sitwell

Making money is a hobby that will complement any other hobbies you have, beautifully.
Scott Alexander

My only hobby is laziness, which naturally rules out all others.
Anonymous

A hobby is only fun if you do not have time to do it.
Leo Beenhakker

Beware the hobby that eats.
Benjamin Franklin

Home

There's no place like home.
Judy Garland [in the movie The Wizard of Oz*]*

You Can't Go Home Again.
Thomas Wolfe [title of book]

There is nothing like staying at home for real comfort.
Jane Austen

Home is the place where, when you have to go there, they have to take you in.
Robert Frost

The way to cure homesickness is to go home.
Edna Ferber

Home is not where you live, but where they understand you.
Christian Morganstern

Home is a place you grow up wanting to leave, and grow old wanting to get back to.
John Ed Pearce

Home is where you can say anything you please, because nobody pays any attention to you anyway.
Joe Moore

Every day is a journey, and the journey itself is home.
Matsuo Basho

To feel at home, stay at home.
Clifton Fadiman

You can never go home again, but the truth is you can never leave home, so it's all right.
Maya Angelou

A good home must be made, not bought.
Joyce Maynard

A house that does not have one worn, comfy chair in it is soulless.
May Sarton

Hope

Hope is the feeling you have that the feeling you have isn't permanent.
Mignon McLaughlin [also attributed to Jean Kerr, among others]

The important thing is not that we can live on hope alone, but that life is not worth living without it.
Harvey Milk

While I breathe, I hope.
Medieval proverb

Hope for the best but prepare for the worst.
English proverb

Hope is a very unruly emotion.
Gloria Steinem

Don't ever lose hope. It works.
Jewel

If it were not for hope, the heart would break.
Thomas Fuller

Something will turn up.
Benjamin Disraeli

Houseguests See Entertaining

Humility (or Not)

Life is a long lesson in humility.
J. M. Barrie

Don't be humble—you're not that great.
Golda Meir

Humility is no substitute for a good personality.

Fran Lebowitz

Sometimes I amaze myself. I say this humbly.

Don King

When you've got it, flaunt it.

George Lois

I am so clever that sometimes I don't understand a single word of what I am saying.

Oscar Wilde

A man wrapped up in himself makes a very small bundle.

Benjamin Franklin

If I only had a little humility, I would be perfect.

Ted Turner

Humility is like underwear, essential, but indecent if it shows.

Helen Nielsen

Some people are born on third base and go through life thinking they hit a triple.
Barry Switzer

We are all worms, but I do believe that I am a glow-worm.
Winston Churchill

You probably wouldn't worry about what people think of you if you could know how seldom they do.
Olin Miller

Impatience See Patience (or Not)

Inspiration See Creativity & Inspiration

Insomnia See Sleep & Sleeping

Insults & Name-calling See also Dumb...Dumber...Dumbest

[He has] the integrity of a hyena and the style of a poison toad.
Hunter Thompson

Thou art a boil.
William Shakespeare

He had delusions of adequacy.
Walter Kerr

He has all the virtues I dislike and none of the vices I admire.
Winston Churchill

Little things affect little minds.
Benjamin Disraeli

I was underwhelmed.
George S. Kaufman

He is so good that he is good for nothing.
Italian proverb

His mother should have thrown him away and kept the stork.
Mae West

There are only two things I dislike about her—her face.
Anonymous

Some cause happiness wherever they go; others, whenever they go.

Oscar Wilde

The loud laugh that spoke the vacant mind.

Oliver Goldsmith

Deep down he's shallow.

Anonymous

Your mother was a hamster and your father smelt of elderberries!

John Cleese [in the movie Monty Python and the Holy Grail]

I've had a perfectly wonderful evening. But this wasn't it.

Groucho Marx

He loves nature in spite of what it did to him.

Forrest Tucker

She's nutty as squirrel poo.

J. K. Rowling

He's...*vin ordinaire.*

Anonymous

He has no more backbone than a chocolate éclair.

Theodore Roosevelt

...She's got an IQ somewhere between a brick and a houseplant.

Stanley Bing

Internet

Needless to say, we didn't have Facebook growing up...we had phonebook.

Betty White

On the internet, nobody knows you're a dog.

Peter Steiner

The internet is just a world passing around notes in a classroom.

Jon Stewart

Getting information off the internet is like taking a drink from a fire hydrant.

Mitch Kapor

The internet is so big, so powerful and pointless that for some people it is a complete substitute for life.

Andrew Brown

My favorite thing about the internet is that you get to go into the private world of real creeps without having to smell them.

Penn Jillett

The internet is the most important single development in the history of human communication since the invention of call-waiting.

Dave Barry

A blogger is constantly looking over his shoulder, for fear that he is not being followed.

Robert Brault

There are three kinds of death in this world. There's heart death, there's brain death, and there's being off the network.

Guy Almes

The trouble with the internet is that it's replacing masturbation as a leisure activity.

Patrick Murray

A blogger is an average person who happens to have a need to count his friends every half hour.

Robert Brault

The internet is the trailer park for the soul.

Marilyn Manson

If Al Gore invented the internet, I invented spell check.

Dan Quayle

The day I made that statement, about inventing the internet, I was tired because I'd been up all night inventing the camcorder.

Al Gore

Jealousy

Jealousy can be as cruel as death.

Italian proverb

Love creates jealousy, then jealousy destroys love.

Anonymous

O, beware, my lord, of jealousy. It is the green-eyed monster which doth mock the meat it feeds on.
William Shakespeare

Jealousy is all the fun you *think* they had.
Erica Jong

Being with an insanely jealous person is like being in the room with a dead mammoth.
Mike Nichols

It is not love that is blind, but jealousy.
Lawrence Durrell

Jobs & Work See *also* Bummer—Fired!

The trouble with work is it's so daily.
Anonymous

I think that maybe in every company today there is always at least one person who is going crazy slowly.
Joseph Heller

Few great men could pass Personnel.
Paul Goodman

No man ever listened himself out of a job.
Calvin Coolidge

They say hard work never hurt anybody, but I figure why take the chance.
Ronald Reagan [also attributed to Charlie McCarthy/Edgar Bergen]

The only way to enjoy life is to work. Work is much more fun than fun.
Noël Coward

The trouble with the rat race is that even if you win, you're still a rat.
Lily Tomlin

One of the signs of an approaching nervous breakdown is the belief that one's work is terribly important.
Bertrand Russell

To love what you do and feel that it matters—how could anything else be more fun?
Katharine Graham

I used up all my sick days so I called in dead.
Anonymous

You can't be really first-rate at your work if your work is all you are.
Anna Quindlen

Nothing works unless you do.
Maya Angelou

Never burn bridges. Today's junior prick, tomorrow's senior partner.
Sigourney Weaver [in the movie Working Girl*]*

It's a recession when your neighbor loses his job; it's a depression when you lose yours.
Harry S Truman [also attributed to Dave Beck]

Work expands so as to fill the time available for its completion.
C. Northcote Parkinson

In time, every post tends to be occupied by an employee who is incompetent to carry out its duties.
Laurence J. Peter

It's not so much how busy you are, but why you are busy. The bee is praised; the mosquito is swatted.
Marie O'Conner

[In meetings] Say as little as possible while appearing to be awake.

William P. Rogers

Job Applications & Interviews

The closest anyone ever comes to perfection is on a job application form.

Anonymous

There aren't many job interviews where there's a chance you'll end up naked at the end of it.

Jerry Seinfeld [on the difference between a date and a job interview]

When you go in for a job interview, I think a good thing to ask is if they ever press charges.

Jack Handey

Joy See Happiness & Joy

Jury Duty See Bummer—Jury Duty

Karma

As you sow, so shall you reap.
Bible

Karma is the web of life, the total pattern
of cause and effect.
Clarence Pedersen

Give to the world the best you have, and
the best will come back to you.
Madeleine Bridges

There's no such thing as a free lunch, at
least on a karmic level.
Joan Vinge

How people treat you is their karma; how
you react is yours.
Wayne Dyer

Like gravity, karma is so basic we often
don't even notice it.
Sakyong Mipham

You're not the karma police.
Joan Duncan Oliver

Kids *See* **Children**

Kindness

Be ye kind to one another.
Bible

Always be kind, for everyone is fighting a harder battle.
Plato

The highest form of wisdom is kindness.
Talmud

I have always depended on the kindness of strangers.
Tennessee Williams [in the play A Streetcar Named Desire]

My religion is very simple. My religion is kindness.
Dalai Lama

If you can't be kind, at least be vague.
Miss Manners [aka Judith Martin]

Lawsuits See Bummer—Lawsuits

Laziness

Laziness is nothing more than the habit of resting before you get tired.
Jules Renard

How beautiful it is to do nothing and then rest afterward.
Spanish proverb

There's never enough time to do all the nothing you want.
Bill Watterson

I like the word *indolence*. It makes my laziness seem classy.
Bern Williams

Leaders & Leadership

Leadership, like swimming, cannot be learned by reading about it.
Henry Mintzberg

Leadership is action, not position.
D. H. McGannon

To lead people, walk behind them.
Lao-tzu

Leadership means not giving orders to others, but giving of yourself.
East African tribal proverb

Being responsible sometimes means pissing people off.
Colin Powell

If you don't want to get tackled, don't carry the ball.
Ann McKay Thompson

Lies & Liars

I wasn't lying. I was writing fiction with my mouth.
Homer Simpson [in the TV program The Simpsons]

I misspoke.
Hillary Clinton

Terminological inexactitude...
Winston Churchill

Everybody has something to conceal.
Humphrey Bogart

The truth is Silly Putty.
Paul Krassner

Any fool can tell the truth, but it requires a man of some sense to know how to lie well.
Samuel Butler

Lying is done with words and also with silence.
Adrienne Rich

I don't mind lying, but I hate inaccuracy.
Samuel Butler

Life & Living

Life is not meant to be easy.
Malcolm Fraser

To live is so startling it leaves time for little else.
Emily Dickinson

Life is better than death, I believe, if only because it is less boring, and because it has fresh peaches in it.

Alice Walker

The only rule is don't be boring and dress cute wherever you go. Life is too short to blend in.

Paris Hilton

Life is a struggle.

Victor Hugo

Life is just a series of trying to make up your mind.

Timothy Fuller

Life is just one damned thing after another.

Elbert Hubbard

It's not true that life is one damn thing after another.... It's one thing over and over.

Edna St. Vincent Millay

Life is too short to learn German.

Richard Porson [among others]

It may be that your sole purpose in life is simply to serve as a warning to others.
Anonymous

Life is what happens to you while you're busy making other plans.
John Lennon [among several others, including Allen Saunders and Betty Talmadge]

Life itself is the proper binge.
Julia Child

Life is a box of chocolates, Forrest. You never know what you're goin' to get.
Sally Fields [in the movie Forrest Gump]

Life is short; live it up.
Nikita Khrushchev

Living is like licking honey off a thorn.
Italian proverb

The difference between playacting and real life is that, in real life, it's always opening night.
Ashleigh Brilliant

You're leaving college now and going out into real life... [and] life is not like college. Real life is like high school.

Meryl Streep

Life is a rock. And a hard place.

Juli Duncan

Life is like a 10-speed bicycle. Most of us have gears we never use.

Charles M. Schulz

Life is a puzzle with most of the pieces missing.

Anonymous

Life is a sexually transmitted disease.

Guy Bellamy

Whether it's the best of times or the worst of times, it's the only time we've got.

Art Buchwald

Here is a test to find out whether your mission on earth is finished: If you're alive, it isn't.

Richard Bach

Not a shred of evidence exists in favor of the idea that life is serious.
Brendan Gill

There is no cure for birth and death save to enjoy the interval.
George Santayana

Life is short and full of blisters.
African-American proverb

What if the hokey-pokey really is what it's all about?
Anonymous

It has begun to occur to me that life is a stage I am going through.
Ellen Goodman

Life's a bitch. You've got to go out and kick ass.
Maya Angelou

Loneliness &/or Solitude

Language has created the word loneliness to express the pain of being alone and the word solitude to express the glory of being alone.

Paul Tillich

The happiest of all lives is a busy solitude.

Voltaire

I have been one acquainted with the night.

Robert Frost

I want to be alone.

Greta Garbo [in the movie Grand Hotel, *though the original quote is slightly different. Garbo later commented, "I never said, 'I want to be alone.' I only said, 'I want to be left alone.' There is all the difference."]*

People fighting their aloneness will do almost anything to avoid silence.

Myrtle Barker

I never found the companion that was as companionable as solitude.

Henry David Thoreau

Loneliness adds beauty to life. It puts a special burn on sunsets and makes night air smell better.
Henry Rollins

The dread of loneliness is greater than the fear of bondage, so we get married.
Cyril Connolly

If you are afraid of being lonely, don't try to be right.
Jules Renard

People are lonely because they build walls instead of bridges.
Joseph F. Newton

People drain me, even the closest of friends, and I find loneliness to be the best state in the union to live in.
Margaret Cho

Skillful listening is the best remedy for loneliness, loquaciousness, and laryngitis.
William Arthur Ward

What a lovely surprise to discover how unlonely being alone can be.
Ellen Burstyn

One of the great necessities in America is to discover creative solitude.
Carl Sandburg

I don't like to be labeled as lonely just because I am alone.
Delta Burke

Solitude is pleasant. Loneliness is not.
Anna Neagle

Love & Loving

The heart has its reasons which reason does not understand.
Blaise Pascal

Absence makes the heart grow frantic, not fonder.
Judith Viorst

One is very crazy when in love.
Sigmund Freud

I don't have a love life. I have a like life.
Lorrie Moore

Love liberates everything.
Maya Angelou

Real love is when you don't have to tell each other.
French proverb

I may not be a smart man, but I know what love is.
Tom Hanks [in the movie Forrest Gump*]*

At the touch of love everyone becomes a poet.
Plato

A life lived in love will never be dull.
Leo Buscaglia

You know it's love when you want to keep holding hands even after you're sweaty.
Anonymous

The thing about love is you can really make an ass of yourself.
Candice Bergen [in the movie Starting Over*]*

If I know what love is, it is because of you.
Herman Hesse

I'm miserable if I'm not in love, and, of course, I'm miserable if I am.
Tallulah Bankhead

Being deeply loved by someone gives you strength, while loving someone deeply gives you courage.
Lao-tzu

Love conquers all except poverty and toothaches.
Mae West

To fear love is to fear life.
Bertrand Russell

Take my breath away.
William Shakespeare

Love can find a way.
Ancient proverb

If love is the answer, could you please rephrase the question?
Lily Tomlin

You know you're in love when you can't fall asleep because reality is finally better than your dreams.
Dr. Seuss

Love consists in this, that two solitudes protect and touch and greet each other.
Rainer Maria Rilke

The course of true love never did run smooth.
William Shakespeare

It takes a year, a full turn of the calendar, to get over losing somebody.
Annie Proulx

Nobody in love has a sense of humor.
S. N. Behrman

We can only learn to love by loving.
Iris Murdoch

I love her and that's the beginning of everything.
F. Scott Fitzgerald

Love is the extremely difficult realization that something other than oneself is real.
Iris Murdoch

What the world really needs is more love and less paperwork.
Pearl Bailey

The magic of first love is our ignorance that it can ever end.
Benjamin Disraeli

Who, being loved, is poor?
Oscar Wilde

Love can smack you like a seagull and pour all over your feet like junk mail.
Daniel Handler

Manners See Etiquette

Marriage

It's the normal people who are getting divorced. Nobody else even bothers to get married.
Jill Clayburgh [in the movie An Unmarried Woman]

Marriage is like the Middle East. There's no solution.

Pauline Collins [in the movie Shirley Valentine*]*

One can't explain one's marriage.

Henry James

With my body, I worship thee.

Medieval marriage vow

To you I give myself, for I am yours.

William Shakespeare

The heart of marriage is memories.

Bill Cosby

A happy marriage is the union of two good forgivers.

Robert Quillen

Marriage is our last, best chance to grow up.

Joseph Barth

Our marriage works because we each carry clubs of equal weight and size.

Paul Newman

I love being married. It's so great to find that one special person you want to annoy for the rest of your life.

Rita Rudner

There is so little difference between husbands you might as well keep the first.

Adela Rogers St. Johns

Husbands are like fires. They go out when unattended.

Zsa Zsa Gabor

Don't marry someone you would not be friends with if there was no sex between you.

William Glasser

Don't marry him until you see how he treats the waitress.

Anonymous

Men with pierced ears are better prepared for marriage—they've experienced pain and bought jewelry.

Rita Rudner

Many marriages would be better if the husband and the wife clearly understood that they are on the same side.

Zig Ziglar

A long marriage is two people trying to dance a duet and two solos at the same time.

Anne Taylor Fleming

More marriages might survive if the partners realized that sometimes the better comes after the worse.

Doug Larson

Sometimes I wonder if men & women really suit each other. Perhaps they should live next door & just visit now and then.

Katharine Hepburn

Like good wine, marriage gets better with age—once you learn to keep a cork in it.

Gene Perret

Only choose in marriage a man whom you would choose as a friend if he were a woman.

Joseph Joubert

What counts in making a happy marriage is not so much how compatible you are, but how you deal with incompatibility.

George Levinger

A happy marriage is a long conversation which always seems too short.

Andre Maurois

One thing you learn in a long marriage is how many sneezes to wait before saying "Bless you."

Robert Brault

Marriage is a wonderful invention; then again, so is a bicycle repair kit.

Billy Connolly

Meals

Eat breakfast like a king, lunch like a prince, and dinner like a pauper.

Adelle Davis

Breakfast

All happiness depends on a leisurely breakfast.

John Gunther

Only dull people are brilliant at breakfast.
Oscar Wilde

The critical period in matrimony is
breakfast time.
A. P. Herbert

Lunch

Ask not what you can do for your country.
Ask what's for lunch.
Orson Welles

Lunch is for wimps.
Oliver Stone

Dinner

Dinner was made for eating, not talking.
William Thackeray

Find me a man who's interesting enough to
have dinner with and I'll be happy.
Lauren Bacall

Never argue at the dinner table, for the
one who is not hungry always gets the best
of the argument.
Voltaire

Strange to see how a good dinner and feasting reconciles everybody.

Samuel Pepys

Memory & Memories

Memory is the diary that we all carry about with us.

Oscar Wilde

Nostalgia isn't what it used to be.

Anonymous

Fancy meeting someone and forgetting you've slept with them. It's not good, is it?

Arthur Smith

One always forgets the most important things, it's the things one can't remember that stay with you.

Alan Bennett

I'm always fascinated by the way memory diffuses fact.

Diane Sawyer

Life is all memory, except for the one present moment that goes by you so quickly you hardly catch it going.

Tennessee Williams

Men

Macho does not prove *mucho*.

Zsa Zsa Gabor

My brain? My second favorite organ.

Woody Allen

Doesn't it feel like you live on the Planet of the Guys?

Kate Clinton

What men really want is a sexually experienced virgin.

Anonymous

There are a lot of women who live with pot-bellied pigs.

Catherine Zeta Jones

Most men are trash.

Sigmund Freud

I like two kinds of men—domestic and imported.

Mae West

Men are like a deck of cards. You'll find the occasional king, but most are jacks.

Laura Swenson

I have yet to hear a man ask for advice on how to combine marriage and a career.

Gloria Steinem

The problem is that God gives men a brain and a penis, and only enough blood to run one at a time.

Robin Williams

If the world were a logical place, men would ride sidesaddle.

Rita Mae Brown

Men have an unusual talent for making a bore out of everything they touch.

Yoko Ono

Men are what their mothers made them.

Ralph Waldo Emerson

Mistakes *See* Uh-Oh

Money

Show me the money!
Cuba Gooding, Jr. [in the movie Jerry Maguire*]*

You Can't Take It with You.
Moss Hart & George S. Kaufman [title of play]

The safe way to double your money is to fold it over once and put it in your pocket.
Kin Hubbard

Creditors have better memories than debtors.
Benjamin Franklin

I'm living so far beyond my income that we may almost be said to be living apart.
e. e. cummings [For you purists, this is very similar to Saki's quote: "I'm living so far beyond my means that we may almost be said to be living apart." Great minds and all that.]

Beware of small expenses. A small leak will sink a great ship.
Benjamin Franklin

I've been rich and I've been poor; rich is better.
Sophie Tucker

Bein' poor never holds stylish people back.
Kin Hubbard

To get back on your feet, miss two car payments.
Anonymous

It is better to *live* rich than to *die* rich.
Samuel Johnson

Gentlemen prefer bonds.
Andrew Mellon

I don't like money, actually, but it quiets my nerves.
Joe Louis

When a fellow says, "It ain't the money, it's the principle of the thing"... it's the money.
Kin Hubbard

Words pay no debts.
William Shakespeare

Borrowing, like scratching, is only good for a while.
Jewish saying

Money can't buy happiness, but neither can poverty.
Leo Rosten

Never invest your money in anything that eats or needs repainting.
Billy Rose

A rich man is nothing but a poor man with money.
W. C. Fields

Goddam money. It always ends up making you blue as hell.
J. D. Salinger

If you want to know what God thinks of money, just look at the people he gave it to.
Dorothy Parker

No one can earn a million dollars honestly.
William Jennings Bryan

The lack of money is the root of all evil.
Mark Twain

Money isn't the most important thing in life, but it's reasonably close to oxygen on the "gotta have it" scale.
Zig Ziglar

I don't care about money. I just want to be wonderful.
Marilyn Monroe

Mornings See Meals—Breakfast; Sleep & Sleeping—Mornings

Mosquitoes See Bummer—Mosquitoes

Movies

Never judge a book by its movie.
J. W. Eagan

They didn't *release* that movie; it escaped.
Samuel Goldwyn

What I've learned is that life is too short
and movies are too long.

Denis Leary

Why should people go out and pay money
to see bad films when they can stay home
and see bad television for nothing?

Samuel Goldwyn

There's no thief like a bad movie.

Sam Ewing

A good film is when the price of the dinner,
the theatre admission, and the babysitter
were worth it.

Alfred Hitchcock

A wide screen just makes a bad film twice
as bad.

Samuel Goldwyn

Film lovers are sick people.

Francois Truffaut

You know what your problem is, it's that
you haven't seen enough movies—all of
life's riddles are answered in the movies.

Steve Martin [in the movie Grand Canyon*]*

Music

Hear, and your soul will live.
Bible

Music is forever; music should grow and
mature with you, following you right on up
until you die.
Paul Simon

There is music in the air, music all around
us, the world is full of it, and you simply
take as much as you require.
Edward Elgar

Without music, life would be an error.
Friedrich Nietzsche

Modern music is as dangerous as cocaine.
Pietro Mascagni

Why waste money on psychotherapy when
you can listen to the B Minor Mass?
Michael Torke

If in the afterlife, there is not music, we will
have to import it.
Doménico Cieri Estrada

Life can't be all bad when for ten dollars
you can buy all the Beethoven sonatas and
listen to them for ten years.
William F. Buckley, Jr.

You can't possibly hear the last movement
of Beethoven's Seventh and go slow.
*Oscar Levant [explaining his way out of a
speeding ticket]*

Music is the shorthand of emotion.
Leo Tolstoy

Music is the medicine of the breaking
heart.
Leigh Hunt

I worry that the person who thought up
Muzak may be thinking up something else.
Lily Tomlin

Opera is where a guy gets stabbed in the
back, and instead of dying, he sings.
Robert Benchley

Hell is full of musical amateurs.
George Bernard Shaw

Country music is three chords and the truth.
Harlan Howard

Let us make a joyful noise....
Bible

Name-calling See Insults & Name-calling

Naps See Sleep & Sleeping—Naps

Nature

Nature, as we know her, is no saint.
Henry David Thoreau

Grass is hard and lumpy and damp, and full of dreadful black insects.
Oscar Wilde

I like trees because they seem more resigned to the way they have to live than other things do.
Willa Cather

There is no gravity. The earth sucks.
Anonymous

A bird doesn't sing because it has an answer, it sings because it has a song.
Lou Holtz

Nature is whole and yet never finished.
Goethe

There are no passengers on Spaceship Earth. We are all crew.
Marshall McLuhan

Great things are done when men and mountains meet. This is not done by jostling in the street.
William Blake

Remain true to the earth.
Friedrich Nietzsche

I think it pisses God off if you walk by the color purple in a field somewhere and don't notice it.
Alice Walker

Nature does not hurry, yet everything is accomplished.
Lao-tzu

Hurt not the earth, neither the sea, nor the trees.
Bible

The world is mud-luscious and puddle-wonderful.
e. e. cummings

Nights See Sleep & Sleeping—Nights

Parenthood See Children—Parents & Parenthood

Parking See Bummer—Parking

Parties See Dining Out; Entertaining

Passion See Sex & Passion

Past See also Future

The past is never dead. It's not even past.
William Faulkner

Those who cannot remember the past are condemned to repeat it.
George Santayana

The past is a foreign country; they do things differently there.
Leslie Poles Hartley

You have to know the past to understand the present.
Carl Sagan

I think we all agree, the past is over.
George W. Bush

What's past is prologue.
William Shakespeare

Patience (or Not)

He's run everybody's patience out, and if he'd been on fire, not a soul would have pissed on him to save him.
Rayna Green

They also serve who only stand and wait.
John Milton

Patience and time conquer all things.
Pierre Corneille

Patience is sometimes not being able to think of anything to do.
Anonymous

A gardener does not pull up his flowers each morning to inspect the roots.
Dean Acheson

I am extraordinarily patient, provided I get my own way in the end.
Margaret Thatcher

Have patience. All things are difficult before they become easy.
Saadi

Lack of pep is often mistaken for patience.
Kin Hubbard

Never run after a bus or a man. There will always be another one.
Anonymous

Patience is the ability to idle your motor when you feel like stripping your gears.
Barbara Johnson

Peace See War & Peace

Periods See Bummer—Periods/PMS

Pets See Animals

Persistence See Determination & Persistence

Plumbing Problems See Bummer—
Plumbing Problems

PMS See Bummer—Periods/PMS

Politics & Politicians

The job of a citizen is to keep his mouth
open.
Günter Grass

If God had wanted us to vote, he would
have given us candidates.
Jay Leno

What Washington needs is adult
supervision.
Barack Obama

A billion here, a billion there, and pretty soon you're talking about real money.
Everett Dirksen [U.S. Senator]

Politics is a blood sport.
Aneurin Bevan

The illegal we do immediately. The unconstitutional takes a little longer.
Henry Kissinger

You can fool too many of the people too much of the time.
James Thurber

Politics is far more complicated than physics.
Albert Einstein

A bad politician is one you disagree with.
Winston Churchill

Politics offers yesterday's answers to today's problems.
Marshall McLuhan

A fool and his money are soon elected.
Will Rogers

It this any way to run a country?
Lawrence O'Brien

True terror is to wake up one morning
and discover that your high school class is
running the country.
Kurt Vonnegut

Pregnancy See Children—Pregnancy

Problems (in general) See also Bummer

There is a great disturbance in the Force.
Alec Guinness [in the movie Star Wars: The
Empire Strikes Back*]*

Houston, we have a problem.
Tom Hanks [in the movie Apollo 13*]*

We're all fucked. It helps to remember
that.
George Carlin

These are the times that try men's souls.
Thomas Paine

Life ain't been no crystal stair.
Langston Hughes

Real problems have no solutions.
Anonymous

No matter how bad things get, you've got to go on living, even if it kills you.
Sholem Aleichem

Problems are messages.
Shakti Gawain

The other day a dog peed on me. A bad sign.
H. L. Mencken

If you are going through hell, keep going.
Winston Churchill

I always get the fuzzy end of the lollipop.
Marilyn Monroe [in the movie Some Like It Hot]

No good deed goes unpunished.
Anonymous [though variously attributed to many, including Oscar Wilde and Claire Booth Luce]

Good things fall apart so better things can fall together.
Marilyn Monroe

The answers are always inside the problem, not outside.
Marshall McLuhan

It is tempting, if the only tool you have is a hammer, to treat everything as if it were a nail.
Abraham Maslow

No problem is so big or so complicated that it can't be run away from.
Charles M. Schulz

If you're not part of the solution, you're part of the problem.
Eldridge Cleaver [For you purists, Cleaver's actual words were "It's been said that today, you're part of the solution or you're part of the problem. There is no more middle ground."]

There are some things so serious you have to laugh at them.
Niels Bohr

There must be quite a few things a hot bath won't cure, but I don't know many of them.
Sylvia Plath

Oh, shit.
[Reputedly the last words on the majority of flight recorders recovered after plane crashes.]

Procrastination

I tell you, we are here on Earth to fart around, and don't let anybody tell you different.
Kurt Vonnegut

I love deadlines. Especially the whooshing sound they make as they pass by.
Douglas Adams

In delay lies no plenty.
William Shakespeare

The way to get started is to quit talking and begin doing.
Walt Disney

Don't put off for tomorrow what you can do today, because if you enjoy it today you can do it again tomorrow.
James Michener

Procrastination is the thief of time.
Edward Young

The secret of getting ahead is getting
started.
Sally Berger

Punctuality

If a thing's worth doing, it's worth doing
late.
Frederick Oliver

If you're there before it's over, you're on
time.
Jimmy Walker

Those who are late will be punished by
life itself.
Mikhail Gorbachev

Punctuality is the virtue of the bored.
Evelyn Waugh

Better three hours too soon than a minute
too late.
William Shakespeare

Rejoinders & Replies

Remember what you said, because in a
day or two, I'll have a witty and blistering
retort! You'll be devastated THEN!
Bill Watterson [in Calvin & Hobbes *comic strip]*

Well, la-dee-da!
Diane Keaton [in the movie Annie Hall*]*

Go ahead. Make my day.
Clint Eastwood [in the movie Sudden Impact*]*

No way, dude.
Mike Myers [in the movie Wayne's World*]*

I'll be back.
Arnold Schwarzenegger [in the movie The
Terminator*]*

Been there. Done there.
David Genser

Relationships *See also* **Friends & Enemies;
Marriage;** *etc.*

I felt it shelter to speak to you.
Emily Dickinson

You want monogamy, marry a swan.
Steven Hill [in the movie Heartburn]

Men and women, women and men. It will never work.
Erica Jong

There is no way to take the danger out of human relationships.
Barbara Grizzuti Harrison

Why go out for hamburger when you have steak at home?
Paul Newman

Men are from earth. Women are from earth. Deal with it.
Anonymous

I can't mate in captivity.
Gloria Steinem

The best way to hold a man is in your arms.
Mae West

Just remember that every relationship starts with a one-night stand.
Anthony Edwards [in the movie The Sure Thing]

Sometimes you have to get to know someone really well to realize you're really strangers.

Mary Tyler Moore

Let there be spaces in your togetherness.

Kahlil Gibran

Religion & Spirituality

I considered atheism, but there weren't enough holidays.

Anonymous

We are not human beings trying to be spiritual. We are spiritual beings trying to be human.

Jacquelyn Small

Many are saved from sin by being so inept at it.

Mignon McLaughlin

Why is it when we talk to God, we're said to be praying—but when God talks to us, we're schizophrenic?

Lily Tomlin [also attributed to Thomas Szasz]

Joy is not merely incidental to your spiritual quest. It is vital.

Rebbe Nachman of Breslov

I don't believe in God, but I'm very interested in her.

Arthur C. Clarke

If God doesn't like the way I live, let him tell me, not you.

Anonymous

Restaurants See Dining Out

Revenge

If thine enemy wrong you, buy each of his children a drum.

Chinese proverb

Don't go looking for a fight—but if you're hit, deck the bastard.

Roger Ailes

You can never get ahead of someone by trying to get even with him.

Anonymous

When you go out to seek revenge, dig two graves.
Chinese proverb

Revenge is sweet and not fattening.
Alfred Hitchcock

No more tears now; I will think about revenge.
Mary, Queen of Scots

Risk & Chance

Leap before you look.
Slavic proverb

And the trouble is, if you don't risk anything, you risk even more.
Erica Jong

If you worried about falling off the bike, you'd never get on.
Lance Armstrong

The only difference between a rut and a grave is their dimensions.
Ellen Glasgow

Nothing will ever be attempted, if all possible objections must first be overcome.
Samuel Johnson

You must do the thing you think you cannot do.
Eleanor Roosevelt

You can't steal second if you don't take your foot off first.
Mike Todd

Dare to be naïve.
R. Buckminster Fuller

If you are never scared, embarrassed, or hurt, it means you never take chances.
Julia Soul

You'll always miss 100% of the shots you don't take.
Wayne Gretsky

One cannot leap a chasm in two leaps.
Winston Churchill

You must take your chance.
William Shakespeare

He who is not courageous enough to take risks will accomplish nothing in life.

Muhammad Ali

A ship in harbor is safe, but that is not what ships are built for.

John A. Shedd

The only way of discovering the limits of the possible is to venture a little way past them into the impossible.

Arthur C. Clarke

Chance favors the prepared mind.

Louis Pasteur

Sadness

Laugh and the world laughs with you; weep, and you weep alone.

Ella Wheeler Wilcox

Noble deeds and hot baths are the best cures for depression.

Dodie Smith

I am in desolation and my eyes are large with needing weeping and I have a flush from feverish feeling.
Gertrude Stein

Sorrow makes us all children again.
Ralph Waldo Emerson

It is such a secret place, the land of tears.
Antoine de Saint-Exupéry

Been Down So Long, It Looks Like Up to Me.
Richard Farina [title of book]

You cannot prevent the birds of sadness from passing over your head, but you can prevent their making a nest in your hair.
Chinese proverb

If you have tears, prepare to shed them now.
William Shakespeare

School *See* **Education**

Sex & Passion

Flies spread disease. So keep yours zipped.
Anonymous

I wasn't kissing her. I was just whispering in her mouth.
Chico Marx

Whoever named it necking was a poor judge of anatomy.
Groucho Marx

It's not the size of the ship; it's the size of the waves.
Little Richard

Wild nights! Wild nights! Were I with thee, wild nights should be our luxury!
Emily Dickinson

One person's safe sex is another's abstinence.
Alice Kahn

Sex is the most fun you can have without laughing.

Leo Rosten [and Woody Allen, and many others... a common thought, apparently]

The only people who make love all the time are liars.

Louis Jourdan [in the movie Gigi]

Sex is never an emergency.

Elaine Pierson

Not tonight, Josephine.

Napoleon [supposedly; also a 1911 song title]

I've been in more laps than a napkin.

Mae West

I'm as pure as the driven slush.

Tallulah Bankhead

Women need a reason to have sex. Men just need a place.

Billy Crystal

I love sex. It's free and doesn't require special shoes.

Anonymous

Shopping

Hope springs eternal in a shopper who looks for a ripe cantaloupe.
Anonymous

Whoever said money can't buy happiness simply didn't know where to go shopping.
Bo Derek

Star Trek characters never go shopping.
Doug Coupland

Shopping is better than sex. At least if you're not satisfied, you can exchange it for something you really like.
Adrienne Gusoff

Anyone who lives within their means suffers from a lack of imagination.
Oscar Wilde

People don't buy for logical reasons. They buy for emotional reasons.
Zig Ziglar

Nowadays people know the price of everything and the value of nothing.
Oscar Wilde

I always say shopping is cheaper than a psychiatrist.
Tammy Faye Bakker

If you change lines, the one you just left will start to move faster than the one you are now in.
O'Brian's Law

If men liked shopping, they'd call it research.
Cynthia Nelms

Nothing heals a heavy heart better than a heavy shopping bag.
Anonymous

I bet deep down you still wish your mom would take you clothes shopping every August for the new school year.
Bridget Willard

Sickness See Health

Silence

The things I never say never get me into trouble.
Calvin Coolidge

Silence gives consent.
Oliver Goldsmith

Drawing on my fine command of the language, I said nothing.
Robert Benchley

A closed mouth gathers no feet.
Anonymous

The best friends are those who know how to keep the same silences.
Fulton J. Sheen

Nothing is more useful than silence.
Menander

Be silent and safe—silence never betrays you.
John Boyle O'Reilly

Do not speak unless you can improve the silence.
Proverb

Better to remain silent and be thought a fool than to speak out and remove all doubt.
Abraham Lincoln

Our lives begin to end the day we become silent about things that matter.
Martin Luther King, Jr.

Silence has wonderful creative power.
Anonymous

The quieter you become the more you can hear.
Ram Dass

Simplicity *See also* Clutter

Our life is frittered away by detail....
Simplicity, simplicity, simplicity....
Henry David Thoreau

Simple is good.
Jim Henson

Beware the barrenness of a busy life.
Socrates

The wisdom of life consists of the elimination of nonessentials.
Lin Yutang

I have a simple philosophy. Fill what's empty. Empty what's full. And scratch where it itches.

Alice Roosevelt Longworth

It is far more difficult to be simple than to be complicated.

John Ruskin

You can't have everything, even in California.

Raymond Chandler

In the midst of this chopping sea of civilized life... Simplify, simplify.

Henry David Thoreau

Seek simplicity and distrust it.

Alfred North Whitehead

Life is really simple, but we insist on making it complicated.

Confucius

There must be more to life than having everything!

Maurice Sendak

Remember that the most beautiful things in the world are the most useless; peacocks and lilies, for example.

John Ruskin

Simplicity is making the journey of this life with just baggage enough.

Anonymous

Singlehood *See also* Bummer—Bad Dates

Most single men don't even live like people. They live like bears with furniture.

Rita Rudner

I think, therefore I'm single.

Liz Winston

When I'm alone, I can sleep crossways in bed without an argument.

Zsa Zsa Gabor

A bachelor gets tangled up with a lot of women in order to avoid getting tied up by one.

Helen Rowland

It's like magic. When you live by yourself, all your annoying habits are gone!

Merrill Markoe

I love being single. It's almost like being rich.

Sue Grafton

My knight in shining armor turned out to be a loser in aluminum foil.

Anonymous

I'm single because I was born that way.

Mae West

If you are single there is always one thing you should take out with you on a Saturday night: your friends.

Sarah Jessica Parker [in the TV program Sex and the City*]*

Sometimes you have to stand alone to prove that you can still stand.

Anonymous

Sleep & Sleeping

Mornings

Smile first thing in the morning. Get it over with.

Anonymous

The average, healthy, well-adjusted adult gets up at 7:30 in the morning feeling just plain awful.

Jean Kerr

Early morning cheerfulness can be extremely obnoxious.

William Feather

Early risers, as a rule, are a notably arrogant set.

Walter Dwight

It was such a lovely day I thought it was a pity to get up.

W. Somerset Maugham

The day will happen whether or not you get up.

John Ciardi

Evenings

Whoever thinks of going to bed before twelve o'clock is a scoundrel.

Samuel Johnson

…and so to bed.

Samuel Pepys

Nights

Don't try to solve serious matters in the middle of the night.

Philip K. Dick

Naps

No day is so bad it can't be fixed with a nap.

Carrie Snow

Regular naps prevent old age, especially if you take them while driving.

Anonymous

Not Enough

No matter how big or soft or warm your bed is, you still have to get out of it.

Grace Slick

The amount of sleep required by the average person is just 5 minutes more.
Anonymous

Not being able to sleep is terrible. You have the misery of having partied all night...without the satisfaction.
Lynn Johnston [in the comic strip For Better or For Worse]

Dreaming

Nothing is so boring as listening to someone else describe a dream.
George Carlin

People who don't have nightmares don't have dreams.
Robert Paul Smith

Snoring

Laugh and the world laughs with you, snore and you sleep alone.
Anthony Burgess

Smoking

Pros

I have made it a rule never to smoke more than one cigar at a time.

Mark Twain

A nonsmoker is forced to find food, but for a smoker, breakfast can be a cigarette and a cup of bad coffee.

Brock Fiant

It has always been my rule never to smoke when asleep, and never to refrain when awake.

Mark Twain

Cons

A person's right to smoke ends where the next person's nose begins.

Anonymous

If we see you smoking, we will assume you are on fire and take appropriate action.

Douglas Adams

A smoking section in a restaurant makes as much sense as a peeing section in a swimming pool.
Anonymous

Do you mind if I don't smoke?
Groucho Marx

Snoring   See Sleep & Sleeping—Snoring

Solitude   See Loneliness &/or Solitude; *see also* Singlehood

Spirituality   See Religion & Spirituality

Sports   *See also* Exercise

The moment of victory is much too short to live for that and nothing else.
Martina Navratilova

Baseball

It ain't over 'til it's over.
Yogi Berra

Baseball is like church. Many attend, few understand.

Leo Durocher

Basketball

I look at the NBA as a football game without the helmet.

Tom Tolbert

Boxing

Boxing is show business with blood.

David Belasco

Fishing

Fishing is boring, unless you catch an actual fish, and then it is disgusting.

Dave Barry

There's a fine line between fishing and standing on the shore looking like an idiot.

Steven Wright

Football

Football combines the two worst features of American life. It is violence punctuated by committee meetings.

George Will

If a man watches three football games in a row, he should be declared legally dead.

Erma Bombeck

Golf

You learn very little about golf from life, but you learn a lot about life from golf.

Earl Woods [Tiger's dad]

I could never believe in a game where the one who hits the ball least wins.

Winston Churchill

Jogging

Exactly how intricate a sport is jogging? You were two years old; you ran after the cat; you pretty much had it mastered.

Rick Reilly

The first time I see a jogger smiling, I'll consider it.

Joan Rivers

The only reason I'd take up jogging is so I could hear heavy breathing again.

Erma Bombeck

Lacrosse

They thought *lacrosse* was what you did in *la church.*

Robin Williams

Skiing

I do not participate in any sport with ambulances at the bottom of a hill.

Erma Bombeck

Swimming

Swimming good for the figure? Did you ever get a good look at a whale?

Anonymous

Tennis

No one is more sensitive about his game than a weekend tennis player.
Jimmy Cannon

Stress

I'm not [biting my fingernails]. I'm biting my knuckles. I finished the fingernails months ago.
Joseph Mankiewicz

There cannot be a crisis next week. My schedule is already full.
Henry Kissinger

What does not destroy me, makes me stronger.
Friedrich Nietzsche

In times of stress, be bold and valiant.
Horace

I've tried yoga, but I find stress less boring.
Anonymous

For fast-acting relief, try slowing down.
Lily Tomlin

Is everything as urgent as your stress would imply?

Carrie Latet

Success & Failure

Success

The *Eagle* has landed.

Neil Armstrong

Success comes before work only in the dictionary.

Anonymous

Now that I'm here, where am I?

Janis Joplin

Success didn't spoil me. I've always been insufferable.

Fran Lebowitz

The road to success is always under construction.

Arnold Palmer

Whom the gods wish to destroy they first call promising.

Cyril Connolly

Success is going from failure to failure
without loss of enthusiasm.
Winston Churchill

Failure

If at first you don't succeed, so much for
skydiving.
Anonymous

If at first you don't succeed, failure may be
your style.
Quentin Crisp

If you're gonna be a failure, at least be one
at something you enjoy.
Sylvester Stallone

Failure has no friends.
John F. Kennedy

Success & Failure

I don't know the key to success, but the
key to failure is trying to please everybody.
Bill Cosby

Success is 99 percent failure.
Soichiro Honda

The two hardest things in life to handle are failure and success.

Anonymous

Success has made failures of many men.

Cindy Adams

I'd rather be a failure at something I enjoy than a success at something I hate.

George Burns

Failure is taking the path that everyone else does; success is making your own path.

Anonymous

You always pass failure on the way to success.

Mickey Rooney

Only those who dare to fail greatly can ever achieve greatly.

Robert Kennedy

Taxes See Bummer—Taxes

Technology (in general) *See also* Cell Phones; Computers; Internet

If it works, it's out of date.
Stafford Beer

Are you sure it's plugged in?
Anonymous

It has become appallingly obvious that our technology has exceeded our humanity.
Albert Einstein

The real question is not whether machines think but whether men do.
B. F. Skinner

Technology...the knack of so arranging the world that we need not experience it.
Max Frisch

Technology is so much fun but we can drown in our technology. The fog of information can drive out knowledge.
Daniel Boorstin

Any sufficiently advanced technology is indistinguishable from magic.
Arthur C. Clarke

Men have become the tools of their tools.
Henry David Thoreau

The thing with high-tech is that you always
end up using scissors.
David Hockney

Temptation

Always put off until tomorrow what you
should not do at all.
Anonymous

I can resist everything except temptation.
Oscar Wilde

I used to be Snow White, but I drifted.
Mae West

Lead me not into temptation. I can find the
way myself.
Rita Mae Brown

Nothing makes temptation so easy to
resist as being broke.
Anonymous

Tempt not a desperate man.
William Shakespeare

I sometimes resist temptation, but never mischief.
Joyce Rebeta-Burditt

If you're going to do something wrong, at least enjoy it.
Anonymous

Most people would like to be delivered from temptation but would like it to keep in touch.
Robert Orben

Time

Time is nature's way of keeping everything from happening at once.
Anonymous

There is more to life than increasing its speed.
Gandhi

Time past and time future, What might have been and what has been, Point to one end, which is always present.

T. S. Eliot

All the money in the world doesn't mean a thing if you don't have time to enjoy it.

Oprah Winfrey

Time is a storm in which we're all lost.

William Carlos Williams

Time heals what reason cannot.

Seneca

Three o'clock is always too late or too early for anything you want to do.

Jean-Paul Sartre

Lost time is never found again.

Benjamin Franklin

Time flies, but remember: You are the navigator.

Anonymous

Nothing, of course, begins at the time you think it did.

Lillian Hellman

Traffic   **See** **Driving & Traffic**

Travel & Adventure   **See also** **Bummer—**
Flying

The Good

Follow the yellow brick road.
[in the movie The Wizard of Oz]

No matter what happens, travel gives you
a story to tell.
Jewish proverb

Everything good is on the highway.
Ralph Waldo Emerson

Every step of the journey is the journey.
Zen saying

The detour of course became the actual
path.
Gretel Ehrlich

All adventures, especially into new
territory, are scary.
Sally Ride

Got to move on, got to travel, walk away my blues.

Terry & Renny Russell

A journey of a thousand miles begins with a cash advance.

Anonymous

The Bad

It is always far to go when there are no friends at the end of the journey.

African proverb

She travels grubbiest who travels light.

Erma Bombeck

It's easier to find a traveling companion than to get rid of one.

Peg Bracken [such a truism that many travelers, including Art Buchwald, have made this comment]

The distinguishing mark of true adventures is that it is often no fun at all while they are actually happening.

Kim Stanley Robinson

I spent a year in that town, one Sunday.
Warwick Deeping [also attributed to George Burns]

When you look like your passport photo, it's time to go home.
Erma Bombeck

Truncated Advice

It does not require many words to speak the truth.
Chief Joseph

Listen, everyone is entitled to my opinion.
Madonna

Be of good cheer.
William Shakespeare

Aim for brevity while avoiding jargon.
Edsger Dijkstra

Brevity is the soul of wit.
William Shakespeare

When a thing has been said, and said well, have no scruple. Take it and copy it.

Anatole France

Give credit where credit is due.

American proverb

A lie will go round the world while truth is pulling its boots on.

American proverb

Let me tell the world.

William Shakespeare

Uh-Oh

Toto, I've a feeling we're not in Kansas anymore.

Judy Garland [in the movie The Wizard of Oz*]*

I'm sorry if anyone was offended by the wardrobe malfunction.

Justin Timberlake

Do not fear mistakes. There are none.

Miles Davis

I never make stupid mistakes. Only very, very clever ones.

John Peel

Mistakes are part of the dues one pays for a full life.

Sophia Loren

When she opens her mouth, it's only to change feet.

Anonymous

You will do foolish things, but do them with enthusiasm.

Colette

When weaving a blanket, an Indian woman leaves a flaw in the weaving of that blanket to let the soul out.

Martha Graham

Vegetarians & Vegetarianism

I was a vegetarian until I started leaning toward the light.

Rita Rudner

Animals are my friends... and I don't eat my friends.

George Bernard Shaw

I am not a vegetarian because I love animals; I am a vegetarian because I hate plants.

A. Whitney Brown

Vegetables are interesting but lack a sense of purpose when unaccompanied by a good cut of meat.

Fran Lebowitz

Vegetarian: a person who eats only side dishes.

Gerald Lieberman

A vegetarian in Texas. You're a long way from home.

Lee Child

I did not become a vegetarian for my health. I did it for the health of the chickens.

Isaac Bashevis Singer

Vegetarianism—you are what you eat, and who wants to be a lettuce?

Peter Burns

I am not a *complete* vegetarian. I eat only animals that have died in their sleep.

George Carlin

Who's going to save me from all these vegetarians?

Günter Grass

Visitors See Entertaining

War & Peace

I don't oppose all wars. What I am opposed to is a dumb war.

Barack Obama

War is God's way of teaching Americans geography.

Ambrose Bierce

An unjust peace is better than a just war.

Cicero

A little rebellion now and then is a good thing.
Thomas Jefferson

Ideologies separate us. Dreams and anguish bring us together.
Eugene Ionesco

You can't shake hands with a clenched fist.
Indira Gandhi

War does not determine who is right—only who is left.
Bertrand Russell

Only a peace between equals can last.
Woodrow Wilson

The mere absence of war is not peace.
John F. Kennedy

War is not healthy for children and other living things.
Lorraine Schneider

You don't have to have fought in a war to love peace.
Geraldine Ferraro

Everyone's a pacifist between wars. It's like being a vegetarian between meals.
Colman McCarthy

Draft beer, not people.
Bob Dylan

You can no more win a war than you can win an earthquake.
Jeannette Rankin

Sometime they'll give a war and nobody will come.
Carl Sandburg

Older men declare war. But it is the youth that must fight and die.
Herbert Hoover

You cannot prevent and prepare for war at the same time.
Albert Einstein

If you want to make peace, you don't talk to your friends. You talk to your enemies.
Moshe Dayan

It pays to know the enemy—not least because at some time you may have the opportunity to turn him into a friend.

Margaret Thatcher

Weather

It was a dark and stormy night....

Edward Bulwer-Lytton [and Snoopy, too]

Bad weather always looks worse through a window.

Anonymous

Weather forecast for tonight: dark.

George Carlin

Spring is nature's way of saying, "Let's party!"

Robin Williams

There's no such thing as bad weather, just soft people.

Bill Bowerman

The best thing to do when it's raining is to let it rain.

Henry Wadsworth Longfellow

You can't get mad at weather because weather's not about you. Apply that lesson to most other aspects of life.
Doug Coupland

A lot of people like snow. I find it to be an unnecessary freezing of water.
Carl Reiner

It ain't a fit night out for man or beast.
W. C. Fields [in the movie The Fatal Glass of Beer*]*

Spring is when you feel like whistling even with a shoe full of slush.
Doug Larson

Rain doesn't fall on one roof alone.
Cameroonian proverb

Name the season's first hurricane Zelda and fool Mother Nature into calling it a year.
Robert Brault

Our severest winter, commonly called the spring.
William Cowper

When it rains, it pours.
Anonymous

'Tis bitter cold, and I am sick at heart.
William Shakespeare

There is no such thing as bad weather, only inappropriate clothing.
Ranulph Fiennes

It is best to read the weather forecast before we pray for rain.
Mark Twain

Women

Where there is a woman, there is magic.
Ntozake Shange

There is nothing, nothing, nothing two women cannot accomplish before noon.
Anonymous

Women never have young minds. They are born three thousand years old.
Shelagh DeLaney

At the end of the day, you've got to have the balls to be feminine.
Suzannah Constantine

I'd rather be a woman than a man. Women can cry, they can wear cute clothes, and they're first to be rescued off sinking ships.
Gilda Radner

My advice to the women's clubs of America is to raise more hell and fewer dahlias.
James McNeill Whistler

If you want anything said, ask a man. If you want anything done, ask a woman.
Margaret Thatcher

Words to Live By *See also* Advice—Damned Good Advice

After all, tomorrow is another day.
Vivien Leigh [in the movie Gone with the Wind*]*

Make it so.
Star Trek

Carpe diem.
Horace [If you're fluent in Latin—or loved the movie Dead Poets Society—you'll know this means "Seize the day." However, carpe diem is both shorter and has a bit more flair.]

Ninety percent of everything is crap.
Theodore Sturgeon

Remember, we're all in this alone.
Lily Tomlin

Less is more.
Ludwig Mies van der Rohe

May the Force be with you.
Star Wars

Frankly, my dear, I don't give a damn.
Clark Gable [in the movie Gone with the Wind]

Find a need and fill it.
Ruth Stafford Peale

After ecstasy, the laundry.
Zen saying

Go slowly, breathe and smile.
Thich Nhat Hanh

Truth is always subversive.
Anne Lamott

Be here now.
Ram Dass

Keep on keepin' on.
Anonymous

Live long and prosper.
Mr. Spock [in the TV program Star Trek*]*

Here's looking at you, kid.
Humphrey Bogart [in the movie Casablanca*]*

Work See Jobs & Work

Worry

You can't wring your hands and roll up your sleeves at the same time.
Pat Schroeder

Worriers spend a lot of time shoveling smoke.

Claude McDonald

Wanna fly, you got to give up the shit that weighs you down.

Toni Morrison

Do not anticipate trouble or worry about what may never happen. Keep in the sunlight.

Benjamin Franklin

Worry gives a small thing a big shadow.

Swedish proverb

If a man can remember what he worried about last week, he has a very good memory.

Woody Allen

If you can solve your problem, then what is the need of worrying? If you cannot solve it, then what is the use of worrying?

Shantideva

That's the secret of life—replace one worry with another.

Charles M. Schulz

This too shall pass.

Anonymous

Selected Bibliography

Abel, David W. *What's That You Say? A Collection of Contrasting Quotations*. New York: David Abel, 1990.

Agel, Jerome and Glanze, Walter, compilers. *Pearls of Wisdom*. New York: Collins, 1987.

Andrews, Robert, compiler. *The New Penguin Dictionary of Modern Quotations*. London: Penguin, 2003.

Bartlett's Familiar Quotations. 17th edition. Boston: Little, Brown, 2002.

Beilenson, Evelyn and Ann Tenenbaum. *Wit and Wisdom of Famous American Women*. White Plains, New York: Peter Pauper Press, 1986.

Berk, Sally Ann, editor. *The Big Little Book of Jewish Wit & Wisdom*. New York: Black Dog & Leventhal Publishers, 2000.

Brallier, Jess M., compiler. *Medical Wit and Wisdom*. Philadelphia: Running Press, 1993.

Brilliant, Ashleigh. *Appreciate Me Now and Avoid the Rush*. Santa Barbara, California: Woodbridge Press Publishing, 1981.

Byrne, Robert. *1,911 Best Things Anybody Ever Said*. New York: Fawcett Columbine, 1988.

Camp, Wesley D. *Camp's Unfamiliar Quotations from 2000 B.C. to the Present*. Paramus, New Jersey: Prentice Hall, 1990.

Carlin, George. *Braindroppings*. New York: Hyperion, 1997.

Charlton, James, editor. *The Writer's Quotation Book: A Literary Companion*. Yonkers, New York: Pushcart Press, 1980.

Colombo, John Robert, editor. *Popcorn in Paradise: The Wit and Wisdom of Hollywood*. New York: Holt, Rinehart and Winston, 1979.

Cooper, Karol and Ross, Alan, compilers and editors. *Love Is Forever: A Romantic Ride of Cupid's Arrow*. Nashville, Tennessee: Walnut Grove Press, 1999.

Daley, James, editor. *The Book of Green Quotations*. Mineola, New York: Dover Publications, 2009.

Diagram Group. *The Little Giant Encyclopedia: Toasts and Quotes*. New York: Sterling Innovation, 2009.

Edelstein, Barry. *Bardisms—Shakespeare for All Occasions*. New York: Collins, 2009.

Elliott, Charles, editor. *The Quotable Cat Lover*. New York: Lyons Press, 2000.

Frank, Catherine, editor. *Quotations for All Occasions*. New York: Columbia University Press, 2000.

Fulton, Roger. *Commonsense Management—Quick Wisdom for Good Managers*. Berkeley, CA: Ten Speed Press, 2009.

Handley, Helen and Andra Samelson, editors. *Child— A Literary Companion*. Wainscott, New York: Pushcart Press, 1992.

Henson, Jim. *It's Not Easy Being Green: And Other Things to Consider*. New York: Hyperion Press, 2005.

Humes, James C. *The Wit & Wisdom of Winston Churchill*. New York: HarperPerennial, 1994.

Jakes, Jacqueline. *Sister Wit: Devotions for Women*. Waterville, ME: Thorndike Press, 2002.

Jarman, Colin M. *The Book of Poisonous Quotes*. Chicago: Contemporary Books, 1993.

Jarski, Rosemarie. *Dim Wit—The Stupidest Quotes of All Time*. Berkeley, CA: Ulysses Press, 2010.

Keep Calm and Carry On: Good Advice for Hard Times. Kansas City, MO: Andrews McMeel Publishing, 2009.

Klein, Allen, compiler. *The Change-Your-Life Quote Book*. New York: Portland House, 2001.

Klein, Shelley. *Frankly, My Dear: Quips and Quotes from Hollywood*. Hauppauge, New York: Barron's Educational Series, 2006.

Lankevich, George J., editor. *The Wit and Wisdom of the Talmud: Proverbs, Sayings, and Parables for the Ages*. Garden City Park, NY: SquareOne Classics, 2002.

Latham, Mark. *A Conga Line of Suckholes—Mark Latham's Book of Quotations*. Melbourne: Melbourne University Press, 2006.

Lau, Theodora. *Best-Loved Chinese Proverbs*. 2nd edition. New York: Collins Reference, 2008.

Lloyd, John and John Mitchinson. *If Ignorance Is Bliss, Why Aren't There More Happy People? Smart Quotes for Dumb Times*. New York: Harmony Books, 2008.

Lovric, Michelle. *Women's Wicked Wit, from Jane Austen to Roseanne Barr*. Chicago: Chicago Review Press, 2001.

Mack, Joshua. *Karma 101*. New York: Barnes & Noble Books, 2002.

Mad Magazine Editors, compilers. *MAD—The Half-Wit and Wisdom of Alfred E. Neuman*. New York: Warner Books, 1997.

Magee, Mike. *The Book of Choices: A Treasury of Insights for Personal and Professional Growth*. New York: Spencer Books, 2002.

Makay, Ian, compiler and editor. *Food for Thought.* Freedom, CA: Crossing Press, 1995.

Murray, John A. *The Quotable Nature Lover.* New York: The Lyons Press, 1999.

Nalebuff, Rachel Kauder, editor. *My Little Red Book.* New York: Twelve, 2009.

Partnow, Elaine, compiler and editor. *The New Quotable Woman.* New York: Meridian, 1993.

Peck, M. Scott, editor. *Abounding Faith: A Treasury of Wisdom.* Kansas City, MO: Andrews McMeel Publishing, 2003.

Peter, Laurence. *Peter's Quotations for Our Time.* New York: Bantam, 1977.

Rees, Nigel. *Cassell's Humorous Quotations.* London: Cassell, 2001.

Roney, Carley. *The Knot Guide to Wedding Vows and Traditions: Readings, Rituals, Music, Dances, Speeches, and Toasts.* New York: Broadway Books, 2000.

Rosten, Leo. *Leo Rosten's Carnival of Wit.* New York: Dutton, 1994.

Safire, William, and Safir, Leonard, compilers and editors. *Good Advice.* New York: Wings Books, 1992.

Safire, William, and Safir, Leonard, compilers and editors. *Words of Wisdom: More Good Advice.* New York: Simon & Schuster, 1989.

Safransky, Sy. *Sunbeams: A Book of Quotations.* Berkeley, CA: North Atlantic Books, 1990.

Salwak, Dale, editor. *The Wonders of Solitude.* Novato, CA: New World Library, 1998.

Shapiro, Fred R., editor. *The Yale Book of Quotations.* New Haven: Yale University Press, 2006.

Sherrin, Ned, editor. *The Oxford Dictionary of Humorous Quotations.* Oxford: Oxford University Press, 2005.

Sherwood, Patricia M. *The Quotable Dog Lover.* New York: The Lyons Press, 2000.

Simpson, James B., compiler. *Simpson's Contemporary Quotations.* Boston: Houghton Mifflin, 1988.

Spiegelman, Art and Bob Schneider, editors. *Whole Grains—A Book of Quotations.* New York: Douglas Links, 1973.

Stiel, Holly. *Thank You Very Much.* Berkeley, CA: Ten Speed Press, 1995.

Torricelli, Robert G., editor. *Quotations for Public Speakers—A Historical, Literary, and Political Anthology.* New Brunswick, NJ: Rutgers University Press, 2001.

Venstra, Elizabeth. *True Genius—1001 Quotes That Will Change Your Life.* New York: Skyhorse Publishing, 2008.

Warner, Carolyn. *Treasury of Women's Quotations.* Englewood Cliffs, NJ: Prentice Hall, 1992.

Watkins, Mel, editor. *African American Humor—The Best Black Comedy from Slavery to Today.* Chicago: Lawrence Hill Books, 2002.

Wilde, Oscar. *Oscar Wilde's Wit and Wisdom: A Book of Quotations.* Mineola, NY: Dover Publications, 1998.

Will-Weber, Mark, editor. *The Quotable Runner: Great Moments of Wisdom, Inspiration, Wrongheadedness, and Humor.* New York: Breakaway Books, 1995.

Winokur, Jon, compiler and editor. *The Portable Curmudgeon*. New York: New American Library, 1987.

Winokur, Jon, compiler and editor. *The Portable Curmudgeon Redux*. New York: Dutton, 1992.

Winokur, Jon, compiler and editor. *Zen to Go—Bite-sized Bits of Wisdom*. Seattle: Sasquatch Books, 2005.

Wormell, Christopher, editor and illustrator. *Kitchen Wisdom: A Collection of Savory Quotations*. Philadelphia: Running Press, 1995.

Zadra, Dan, compiler. *I Believe in You*. Edmunds, WA: Compendium, 1999.

Useful Internet Sites

If you google "quotations," over 33 million resources turn up, from general to very, very specific sites. Here are some of the more reliable general collections:

Bartleby Library: Great Books Online
https://www.bartleby.com
Thousands of full-text poems, plays, etc., plus 100,000 quotations. Trustworthy, classic stuff.

The Other Pages
https://www.theotherpages.org/quote.html
Straightforward compilation of 29,000+ entries in 30 collections. Around since 1994, compliments of a dedicated quote hobbyist.

Creative Quotations
https://creativequotations.com
50,000 quotations from 3,000+ famous people.

The Quotations Page
http://quotationspage.com
Oldest quotation site on the Web; 26,000+ quotes.

Quoteland
http://www.quoteland.com
Includes more modern quotes.

Wikiquote
https://en.wikiquote.org
User-created collection, brought to you by the Wikipedia folks.

Other Books from Ulysses Press

THE BIG BOOK OF CRYPTID TRIVIA
Fun Facts and Fascinating Folklore about Bigfoot, Mothman, Loch Ness Monster, the Yeti, and More Elusive Creatures
Bernadette Johnson, $16.95

Explore the world of cryptozoology in this first-ever trivia book all about the folklore, study, and eye-witness testimonies of cryptids like the Jersey Devil, Yeti, and more!

THE BIG BOOK OF SPY TRIVIA
Spy Stories, Secret Agent Facts, and Espionage Skills from History's Greatest Covert Missions
Bernadette Johnson, $14.95

Discover the fascinating true stories of spies and secret agents throughout history in this ultimate collection of espionage trivia.

POCKET HOTTIES: HARRY STYLES
Inspirational Quotes and Observations on Life
Editors of Ulysses Press, $9.99

A collection of all the best quotes from superstar and Grammy award winner Harry Styles, this book will cover his thoughts on relationships, life, fashion and style, success, music, and himself.

POCKET HOTTIES: PEDRO PASCAL
Inspirational Quotes and Observations on Life
Editors of Ulysses Press, $9.99

Funny, inspiring, and entertaining, this quote collection celebrates every endearing quality that actor and internet daddy Pedro Pascal has all in a pocket-sized package!

SERIAL KILLER TRIVIA
Fascinating Facts and Disturbing Details That Will Freak You the F*ck Out
Michelle Kaminsky, $14.95

Discover chilling and mind-blowing facts in this ultimate collection of serial killer trivia for true crime fanatics.

About the Authors

Sayre Van Young, long a research librarian at the Berkeley Public Library, now moonlights as an author, book editor, and indexer. Her previous books include *The Unofficial Harry Potter Vocabulary Builder* and *London's War—A Traveler's Guide to World War II*.

Marin Van Young is a former actress and current advertising copywriter with an affinity for short, punchy quotes and social media. She is the author of *Picture-Perfect Escapes—Charleston*.